THE GIFT OF MERCY

How to Understand Differences *and* Forgive Others

Ed Schwartz

First Edition

Oak Creek Publishing
Bluffton, Indiana

The Gift of Mercy

First Edition Copyright – 2004
by Ed Schwartz

ISBN: 0-931365-18-X

CONTENTS

FOREWORD

PEACE AND HARMONY

Jeni and I recently received a stunning gift from dear friends of ours. It is a large original drawing of a magnificent lion and a beautiful lamb lying together, peacefully, in a grassy meadow. The lamb is nestled next to the lion and they both are the image of contentment. The scene is one of peace and harmony. As you look at the drawing, you think of a perfect world yet to come.

The Bible speaks of that future peaceful world in:

Isaiah 11:6 - The wolf also shall dwell with the lamb, and the leopard shall lie down with the kid; and the calf and the young lion and the fatling together...

This verse creates a word picture not easily forgotten. Most of us dream of the day when peace and harmony will fill the earth and the heavens.

However, the realities of life are not as peaceful or harmonious as Heaven or this drawing. In our current world, nothing is quite as opposite as a wolf and lamb; a leopard and baby goat; or a calf and a lion. How can two extremely different animals live together in tranquil serenity? When God Himself meets the needs of the lion as well as the lamb, there is peace and harmony. God minimizes the differences and the two opposites can co-exist.

REFLECTIONS

As pastor of a congregation for over 20 years, God has given me the opportunity to learn at the feet of many of my brothers and sisters in Christ. That education has been priceless. Those teachings have assisted me in my 35 year marriage to Jeni, as well as with countless other relationships.

7

I have learned most conflicts and relationship problems are rooted in the differences between two unique individuals. When we begin to understand those differences, we can more readily grant grace, mercy and forgiveness to those who hurt us. This book is a study of the major differences between us as unique human beings.

I believe God is the source of healing and His methods are revealed in His book, the Bible. This book, The Gift of Mercy, is not meant to take away from the Scriptures. Rather the principles of this book are derived from Scripture and have been helpful to me and others in my 20 years of counseling.

ACKNOWLEDGMENTS

First of all, I am thankful for the many, many individuals over the years who have shared their hurts, burdens and wounded hearts with me. Those opportunities have served to stretch me far beyond myself into His wisdom and Word.

I am thankful for my special encouragers. You know who you are.

I am thankful for Jodi and her artistic abilities with the lion and lamb.

I am thankful for those dear elders and ministers who have encouraged me in this labor. Their positive reinforcement spurred me on.

I am thankful for my close editor friends who provided careful and tedious checking of the manuscripts for clarity and accuracy.

I am thankful for the wonderful help and love of my wife of 35 years, Jeni; our children and their spouses - Tonia and Doug – Rick and Jen; and the 6+ grandchildren who teach me much about unconditional love.

Last but not least, thanks to the Creator of the universe – the ultimate Healer of wounded hearts.

INTRODUCTION

What do a cracked mirror, someone else's eyeglasses, a dirty car windshield and hurt feelings have in common? All of them provide us with a distorted or incorrect view of reality.

To return a cracked mirror to usefulness, the broken glass must be removed and replaced. To remove the distraction of a dirty car windshield, effort must be made to clean it. Similarly, to mend hurt feelings, special care must be taken to repair the damaged emotions. Hurt comes our way from a multitude of sources and in a variety of shapes and forms. Inevitably, our emotions become involved and tend to distort our view of life. Unless we learn how to remove those hurts, or at the least minimize them, we can have lasting damage.

- **Hurts make us prone to inaction, or inappropriate actions and reactions.**
- **Wounds may cause us to have mistaken priorities and improper motives.**
- **The resulting deception and conflict distorts and damages our relationship with God and others.**
- **We can learn how to handle the inevitable hurts by granting forgiveness and compassion to those who hurt us.**
- **God provides His Word and Holy Spirit to teach us how to forgive others.**
- **Our acts of compassion can bring a new joy to life and pave the way to removing the hurt.**
- **The seemingly impassable void between the hurt and forgiveness is bridged by our understanding of the differences among people.**

In this book along with the chapter 16 workbook, we will seek to identify some of the daily hurts we either receive or give to one another. Those hurts may come from those who are very close to us as family, friends, business associates, as well as from complete strangers.

Hurt feelings, resentment, anger and defensiveness are the symptoms that first identify the emotional hurt that is a part of life. That hurt can either dictate our future in a negative way, or it can add a new dimension to our lives. The hurt can become a grudge and a hatred that can last for years, or it can be reduced to rubble in seconds. When hurt lingers, we have baggage. When we learn how to forgive those who hurt us, we find new meaning to the elusive, abundant life referred to in...

John 10:10: I am come that they might have life, and that they might have it more abundantly.

Together we will follow a process of identifying hurt, reducing and/or forsaking it and moving forward.

- We will search out the magnificent vertical relationship we can have with our Heavenly Father.
- We will seek a better understanding of the ideals of God, as well as the realities of life.
- We will understand how God's ideals and life's realities sometimes seem to collide.
- We will seek to better understand how God values us.
- We will seek to develop a Biblical perspective of God.
- We will focus on a study of the differences which tend to promote conflict among us.
- We will seek to understand how our differences can damage otherwise healthy relationships.

We will be studying the following eight areas which make us uniquely different from each other:

1. Male and female gender
2. Personality characteristics
3. Backgrounds and experiences
4. Spiritual gifts
5. Personal enrichment and fulfillment factors
6. Ways in which we handle emotions
7. Fears
8. Love versus like preferences

The end result will be:

- Knowing God in a richer way.
- Having a deeper and healthier relationship with Him.
- Seeing ourselves in a more honest manner.
- Knowing others in more profound ways.
- Having deeper and more meaningful relationships with each another.

WHERE DO WE START?

Before you start reading Chapter 1, please turn to the workbook on page 179 of Chapter 16 and take the 7 tests. The test results will give you a starting point from which to measure yourself later. When you have finished reading the book, take the tests again and compare the results.

- 1 -

THE REALITY OF LIFE

If we had met yesterday and we had an hour conversation about issues of life, it is conceivable I would have made you uncomfortable a time or two in those sixty minutes. It would not have been my desire to anger or aggravate you, but probably you and I would be different enough that it could have happened.

When I inadvertently said something which hurt you, it might have been difficult for you to grant me mercy since you did not know me. However, if you had read this particular chapter _before_ we had met, it would have been different. You would have been more willing to forgive my button-pushing or lack of discretion, since you would know me better.

This chapter probes into my background and experiences for a very specific purpose. It is an illustration of the realities of life and how they shape us. We all have _realities of life_ we must deal with. Knowing I am normal and have these issues makes it reasonably certain you have issues also. Knowing I want you to forgive my failures and weaknesses because of my issues helps me to understand I should do the same for you.

UNCHANGEABLE BEGINNINGS

On November 6, 1949, I was born in Indiana. I was the biological and genetic combination of a father and a mother. Their genetic traits left their marks on me and within me.

Instilled within me were unique God-given gifts, talents and personality. No one else ever born in the past or arriving on some future day will be just like me. No one else will have the combination of personality, gifts, talents and genetic make-up that were placed within me.

There were things about myself that were irreversible. Being born male, my personality, spiritual gifts, talents, parents, where I lived, whether or not I had siblings and my birth order was all a part of the life of which I had no choice.

The first 17 years of my life had much to do with how my life progressed to the age of 30. At that age, some things happened which changed my life forever. However, the balance of my life is still greatly affected by those first 17 years.

As an illustration about the realities of life, I would like to share some things about myself. My life is not any more traumatic or special than anyone else's. Quite simply, it is the life I can most easily relate to you.

MY DNA...

My genetic makeup predisposed me to certain characteristics:

- I was born with a nose a bit larger than most.
- The Creator provided me with a lanky frame made up of long and lean limbs.
- I was a late-blooming adolescent growing 6 inches and gaining 80 pounds after graduating from high school.
- Genetically, I received a set of lungs that were weaker than normal.
- My personality tended to be rather sensitive, making me vulnerable to emotions that always seemed to be near the surface.

Imagine this child in an elementary school in first grade at the age of five where I was almost the youngest in my class.

During that first year of school, I developed pneumonia, which kept me out of school for six weeks. That set me back in several areas, including those early days of developing friends. As I look back on my twelve years in public school, I was smaller, weaker, shorter and not as bright as most of my peers.

HURTFUL TIMES...

My elementary days were haunted by a class bully. He seemed to have a sole purpose in life of making my life miserable. He was an absolute success! For some reason, he singled me out as the weakling of choice. It seemed he used every opportunity to hurt me, push me, knock me down and laugh at me.

I remember a third grade incident in the school cafeteria when he knocked me down and dared me to get up. By that time, other children in the cafeteria gathered around to see the "fun." (Where were the teachers when you needed them?) I cried and knew if I got up, he would hit me again. I whimpered on the floor, and kids laughed.

After a few years of similar "incidents," I *knew* I was a weak cry-baby. As I looked at myself through my classmates' eyes, I did not like what I saw.

When I was nine years old, my cousins and I were at a city park in the summertime. We had been running and playing tag, and I needed a drink at the water fountain. As I ran up to the water fountain, a group of kids whom I did not know, looked at my bare legs since I was wearing shorts. They started singing, "grand-daddy longlegs, grand-daddy longlegs..." I looked at my legs and realized for the first time in my life that I had long, skinny legs.

Another incident happened about the time I was ten years old. I was in our 1957 two-tone green Pontiac Sky Chief on the way to the local swimming lake. I was in the back seat between two friends with my bare feet on the transmission hump. They started laughing while looking at my feet. They said *"Look at those long feet! You won't be needing skis to water ski!*" That was the first time I realized I had long, skinny feet.

Why would I remember all of those details down to the color of our car and the location on the road after 40 plus years? Hurts have a way of being permanently etched in our minds. Our memories are like a bear trap that simply will not let go!

A year or two later, a friend said my legs looked like two pieces of string with a knot tied in them. Again, letting that memory go would be like telling a pit bull terrier to unlock his jaws.

While in the fourth grade, I disobeyed a teacher and skated on some parking lot ice at recess. I crashed into another student and broke my nose. I previously mentioned my nose was already larger than most. After that, when I looked south, my nose was looking southeast. Thus I had another obvious physical feature that was not normal.

Middle school brought its trauma. I remember a day when we were having physical education in the gymnasium. We were running the dreaded laps around the gym, up and down the stairs, when I got one of those horrible side-aches. I stopped and told the physical education teacher of my pain. He stopped the other boys and pointed to me and said, *"Boys, we have a sissy here who's hurting like a girl."* I am sure those comments were meant to motivate the other boys to extra effort and greater manhood, but it devastated me and made me the brunt of a year long joke.

THE PINNACLE...

By the time I clawed and scraped my way into the senior year, I knew I had finally arrived! I was an upperclassman! I would be respected. I would be esteemed. I was a senior! The end of school was in sight. I would live out my final year there with the honor historically heaped upon the graduating seniors. I was looking forward to the underclassmen looking up to me. Oh, how some expectations are soon dashed on the rocks of reality!

THE ABYSS...

I remember well the experience which occurred when I was barely into my senior year of high school. The incident brought me to an ultimate humiliation and devastated my expectations of honor of being a senior. We would spend the noon hour in the gymnasium playing ping-pong, basketball or just talking. The gym was loaded with freshmen through seniors.

Two of my classmates came up beside me. One picked me up by my right arm, the other by my left. At 5'6" and 120 pounds, what could I do? These two guys were both over 6 feet tall and 200 pounds!

They carried me into the upper bleachers of the gymnasium. (Where were the teachers when you needed them?) They laid me down and stuffed me into the area of the wooden bleachers where you put your feet. Then they sat on me. At the one end, you could see my feet, at the other, my head. It was not long until some students noticed, came to look, and drew the attention of others.

Since I could not move, and because a steady stream of students was coming to look at me, I felt like a corpse at a viewing. I wanted to scream. I wanted to cry. I wanted to hurt my friends. But, I could not even move!

It was at that moment I learned to hate. I hated those who had bullied me during elementary school. I hated those who had hurt me physically or with words. I hated those who had made fun of me and laughed at me. I hated my two classmates for sitting on me. I hated all of the freshmen who laughed at me that day, but the most *devastating* hate of that day was I learned to hate myself.

All of the pent up emotions from twelve years of school came to a boil just under the surface. I suppressed those emotions that day and for the next thirteen years. I pushed those emotions deeper and deeper within me.

MY SUPPORT GROUP

Sometimes people ask me how my life was at home. Mom and Dad listened to my tales of woe from school. They comforted and nurtured me. There were times my parents tried to stop the hurt by going to those in school authority, but that usually only made matters worse. It was comforting to know they tried. However, when I became a tattletale, there were additional consequences with my peers as well.

Basically, my home life was a haven of love, compassion and nurturing. A sad reality of life today is many children are living with torment, abuse, ridicule and rejection and do not have a loving home.

THE CONSEQUENCES

I graduated in the bottom third of my class. Academic excellence was not one of my priorities. Athletically, I was too small to accomplish anything of significance.

All through school, I was generally the last to be picked for any type of team. Having girls chosen before me was not something I could soon forget. When it was my turn to be selected and I was the only one left, the captain would say, "You can go to the other team." It became obvious at that point he would rather have his team complete without me.

I learned to look at myself through other peoples' eyes and through the failures of my life. After years of programming, it ultimately did not matter what people said about me or to me. They did not need to offer their opinions, as I knew their thoughts before they said them, or so I believed. I had begun the long path down the road of deception. My mind was convinced about who and what I was. I did not like what I saw in any way, shape or form. All I saw was someone who was intellectually, physically and emotionally deficient and inferior.

When I got to that point, there was little others could do or say to convince me otherwise. Compliments and positive reinforcement mattered little to me, because I simply did not believe them. I was convinced of who and what I was. Seventeen years of consistent and relentless programming were highly efficient, effective and successful.

When we get to the point of not liking or loving ourselves, we can easily progress to self-hatred. We can make a choice to go down the path of self-destruction, or we develop a compulsive drive of trying to succeed. Both bring about their own style of destruction. Sadly, there are those who simultaneously choose both paths.

The first negative choice is outwardly apparent in the pursuit of all types of addictions. The social workers of our society see these results firsthand. Drugs, alcohol, pornography and sexual issues abound. We hear and see the results of our social ills on the news, and in statistics and polls. They are evident on the streets of America.

The second choice is inwardly negative and not so outwardly apparent. Some of these issues which surface are even acceptable in society today. Though accepted and encouraged, the devastation to relationships and families is nevertheless happening. We become workaholics and seek prestige, wealth or other deceptive rewards. A pursuit of these types of status symbols certainly abounds.

WHICH PATH?

Which path would I take? The temptations were strong. Should I pursue the satisfaction and numbing effect of addictions? Should I seek the fleeting dream of prestige and success? I made a decision when I got out of high school to succeed. I was going to show them! I would really make something of myself. My fear of being rejected ran very deep. Rejection had been my life. The fear of being further rejected by others, as well as a fear of failing, drove me to many wrong attitudes, priorities and motives.

23

THE ULTIMATE ANSWER

Fortunately, God called me to a real relationship with Him shortly after I graduated from high school. I now know if I had not listened to His invitation to serve Him, I would have entered the other path of outward self-destruction. However, in spite of the conversion process of becoming a brand new person in Christ, my school years were still a haunting and shadowy, subconscious part of my past.

The most devastating thing about deception is you do not know when, how or even if it has happened. I had been deceived by all I had been told and come to believe about myself.

One of the most wonderful things about God is He does not want His children enmeshed with deception. He does not give up until we have the opportunity of seeing ourselves as He sees us. I praise God He did not give up on me.

Jeni and I were married in 1969. God brought us together in a wonderful way that strengthened our young faith. Jeni, in many respects, is an opposite of me. She is exactly who God knew I needed. Her insights about life and her way of viewing reality assisted me greatly in my quest for truth about myself. Her patience and mercy were gifts from Him.

SUCCESS BY PRESTIGE

After graduation, I began working for a large corporation and learned a skilled trade. The inner motivation of "needing" to make something of myself took me into management and up the corporate ladder. It took me through some job changes and into an addiction called "workaholism." More hours and more effort provided more income, more prestige and better management positions.

A basic truth of life is that the world will supply money and prestige even when we have wrong motives and priorities. We can generally count on society and the corporate world to reward our efforts. Unfortunately, my impure motives and wrong priorities took their toll on relationships and life in general. Fortunately, God still works in the background.

SUCCESS BY POSSESSIONS

Since the corporate life was going well, I decided we as a family needed to move up in the world. I had always wanted some land with a pond, a creek, a woods and a nice home. Once those things were acquired, the desire for more became stronger. Again, impure motives and wrong priorities took me deeper into the worldly maze of greed and selfishness. Throughout this time, I thought my spirituality was pure. Deception can rob us of many things, but most importantly, it robs us of truth.

My decisions and choices were rooted in my past. I needed to make something of myself. I needed to show "them" I could succeed. I needed to make "them" feel sorry for treating me the way they did. My inappropriate goals in life became a subconscious mind set I never thought about. I simply lived them every minute of every hour of every day for years. It was amazing even thirteen years after graduation, I was not consciously thinking about those days in school. I just lived those years out by being the new "me." Though I was converted and born-again, the Lord was not done molding this lumpy piece of clay.

How can we progress from being stuck in living out our impure motives, wrong priorities and inappropriate attitudes to a point of knowing truth? The next chapter will take us through the recognition of problems and the beginning of the healing process.

- 2 -

HEALING THE WOUNDS

GOOD NEWS?

Pause with me as we listen in on a conversation. The dialogue is between a renowned and respected medical doctor as he visits with a 50 year old elegant, cultured, refined, female patient besieged with a non-healing leg ulcer.

M.D.: I have some good news and I have some bad news. Which would you like to hear first?

Ms.: I would like to hear the good news.

M.D.: Ah, the good news is that I have a cure for your non-healing leg ulcer. We will place a population of *maggots* on your wound to assist in the healing of your ulcer.

Ms: (She faints and does not get to the bad news that conventional antibiotics will not heal the ulcer.)

In 2002, Great Britain reported success in utilizing an unusual method of treatment for some types of wounds. They found some wounds would not respond to conventional dressings and antibiotics. They began to test and use an ancient method of healing - *maggots*. When maggots were applied to some wounds, they would eat the diseased and deadened flesh leaving pink, healthy tissue. By modern standards, this may seem rather bizarre, but it is reportedly highly effective.

Likewise, the issue of dealing with some of our dark and deep emotional wounds requires prompt and intense attention. The process may be hurtful, sickening and revolting, but the healing can save our lives.

TRUTH

I think often of a verse in the Bible which is one of my favorites for several reasons:

John 8:32: And ye shall know the truth, and the truth shall make you free.

Since I suffered from rejection for so many years, I was always very vulnerable to people who would "hurt my feelings." Wounded emotions were a constant part of my life.

Though saved by grace through faith when I was 17, I still needed to be molded and shaped by God. By the age of 30, I had listened to approximately 2,000 sermons since my conversion. Yet, that year, God opened my ears to a specific sermon that touched my heart in a deeper way. A visiting minister gave an unusual diagnosis for my suffering:

When we have hurt feelings, it is an indication of pride in our lives.

Since I suffered nearly daily from hurt feelings, the Holy Spirit grabbed my attention. Surely that statement did not apply to me! It obviously applied to people who came from other families. Most certainly it applied to those who did not have a personal relationship with God. However, the Holy Spirit did not let me off the hook that easily.

To get some rest on the issue, I decided to put the sermon statement to a test. I asked God to reveal truth to me. Over the course of several days, I was saddened to discover there was truth to the statement. I did, in fact, have significant pride in my life. When my feelings were hurt, it was generally because someone did not give me the respect I thought I deserved. Other times, it was because someone did not provide affirmation for something I had done or said. I found out I was a taker and not a giver. I realized I was continually waiting for people to pat me on the back and say, "Well done."

Horror of horrors - the maggots had just been applied to my deep wounds!

When we accept truth in our lives, the Holy Spirit has the opportunity to remove deception. Even though I was learning a new truth, I found out old habits die hard. It was not long afterwards, someone said something to me that was particularly hurtful. I shared it with my pastor, and he said quite simply, "You need to develop broader shoulders and thicker skin." That statement was certainly not what I wanted to hear, but it did have an impact on me as it stirred me to deeper thinking.

A REVELATION
Soon after those occurrences, Jeni and I had the opportunity of joining seven other couples traveling to Haiti on a work team. Seeing great poverty, as well as the devotion and faithfulness of Haitian Believers and missionaries, opened my eyes to who and what I was. My materialistic ways became profoundly evident to me. My priorities in life were under a microscope. My motives for doing good works became glaring contradictions when compared to the mind of Christ.

Those individuals, experiences and circumstances, plus the ever-present power of His Holy Spirit taught me some very basic truths about myself and God. Conviction brought about repentance and a turning around. I learned to compare my motives, priorities, actions and inactions with the Lord's life. I found myself missing the mark significantly. Oh no, more maggots!

The journey since that time has been one of great learning. I have learned much about myself and those around me. I have learned of God's great love for me. The process has not been easy, but I would not trade it for the world. The negative things which happened to me in my younger years were not God's perfect will for my life. As always however, He brought good things from bad.

When we are finally able to break through the deception by His power, He is able to bring good results from bad experiences in spite of who and what we are. The truth is always there, awaiting discovery. He is the guide, and He provides the strength to bring us to His treasury of truth.

CAN HE USE YOU?

Are you among those who have been deeply wounded? Have you experienced tragedy, rejection, failure, grief, disappointment, depression, discouragement, abuse or hurt? Can you see how effective Jesus Christ has been for the world because of his suffering and death? Can you see the effectiveness of Paul, the Apostles, the Disciples, and the early martyrs as they suffered and died? As we remember them, they become an inspiration to us!

I am certain you believe and understand the concept of how we as individuals are programmed by so many situations, circumstances and people. I am sure you see my background has had and will continue to have profound effects on my life. The past has affected my spiritual walk, as well as nearly every emotional part of my being. How thankful I am to know the Holy Spirit of God did not rest until I knew the truth about God's love for me. He has been erasing and or minimizing the effects of those years of rejection and hurt. His love for us knows no bounds. Can God use your hurt, rejection and failures for good?

LEARNING TO DEAL WITH HURT

Dealing with past hurt is complicated and difficult. Those who would call it easy either have not dealt with it personally, or have had only minor scrapes. When we deal with pain, emotions can definitely cloud our vision and cause us to have a distorted view of the reality of life. However, God provides everything for us to get through the tough times. He tells us…

Philippians 4:13: I can do all things through Christ which strengtheneth me.

1 Corinthians 10:13: There hath no temptation taken you but such as is common to man: but God is faithful, who will not suffer you to be tempted above that ye are able; but will with the temptation also make a way to escape, that ye may be able to bear it.

THE PRICE OF HEALING

My vocational background involved designing and producing mechanisms for the manufacturing industry. Designing and building equipment from steel, aluminum, nuts and bolts, motors, cylinders, hydraulics, electronics and pneumatics is a fairly straightforward task. A mechanism is simply a machine, device, tool or implement that can accomplish a task. A mechanism can be as simple as a hammer that pounds in a nail. It can be as complex as a robotic piece of equipment that assembles an automobile. The laws of physics and mechanics can usually predict a successful outcome to designing and building a mechanism.

31

However, developing a mechanism by which we can handle or control emotions is a complicated and difficult chore. To get our fears and emotions under control, we must have courage and resolve. It is not an easy job. Often the effort and resolve required to pursue healing costs us dearly. Speaking of a complicated and difficult task reminds me of something that happened to my wife, Jeni, several years ago...

COURAGE...

Our son, Rick, had a Boa Constrictor snake as a pet. The snake ate mice. Our source for mice was a Fort Wayne, Indiana pet shop 30 miles away. Since Rick did not get there often, the job of bringing mice home went to Jeni as a duty on her shopping trips.

You need to understand three things about Jeni. First, she hates mice. Second, she hates snakes. Third, she loves Rick. Getting hated mice for a hated snake is asking quite a lot from a mom. But, Jeni would do it for Rick. On her drive home with six young mice one particularly stormy night complete with thunder, lightning and rain, the mice chewed a hole in their box and got loose in the car. Can you picture the scene? Ten miles from home, late at night, lightning, thunder, rain, six loose mice in a car with a woman terrified of mice. My brave wife stopped the car along the side of the road in the middle of the storm. I still do not know how she did it, but she captured every one of those mice and got them back into a secure box! Talk about the love of a mother for her son. I was proud of her courage and resolve.

The task of finding a mechanism or tool by which to capture and control complex emotions is no less difficult. It can be done, but is not easy. The task can be summed up with a question:

32

How can I successfully get these hurts behind me and allow God to bring good from them?

The complex and complicated task before us is to learn how to cope with the realities of everyday life by managing and controlling our emotions. We will identify the tools or mechanisms by which we can complete this task. These tools will help us to empathize with others, forgive their trespasses and lack of discretion, as well as to grant mercy to those who hurt us. These mechanisms or tools will help us give the benefit of doubt to others. Simply said, these tools will help us cope with blame, defensiveness, hurt feelings, shame, rejection and failure. Possibly an illustration may assist in learning the HURT / MECHANISM process...

THE HURT...

Permit me to use a personal illustration on how a simple past *hurt* can be brought under control and healed by a "*mechanism.*"

My father was a wonderful dad. He was a kind and loving man who worked hard to support his family. However, as I grew up, there was an area of **hurt** I had experienced in regard to my dad.

He worked full-time in a factory. We also lived on a farm, so when he came home from his work at the factory, his work was not over. He was faced with farming 120 acres, raising pigs, and taking care of 10,000 chickens. I loved to fish, but he rarely had time to take me. When I wanted to go fishing and would ask him to take me, often he would ask an uncle to take me. Even though I loved my uncles and was able to go fishing, I was hurt because I wanted to spend time with my dad.

THE MECHANISM

Years later, it occurred to me that Dad went through the Great Depression (why do they call it Great?). During those years he saw many farms and homes taken from his neighbors and family members because of their inability to make their payments. This obviously caused Dad to have a great desire to get ahead and be prepared for an unpredictable future.

By considering what he went through helped me understand his life. What I perceived as a devotion to work was, in essence, a devotion to his family. When this began to make sense to me, it permitted me the opportunity of letting go of the hurt. Then I developed an admiration and respect for his self-sacrificing lifestyle.

Understanding my dad and trying to walk in his shoes gave me the mechanism by which I could let go of the hurt.

THE HEALING

Many times I have been asked about the tools by which I regained my self-worth after having it stolen from me in those early years. In my life, the healing began when I least expected it and progressed from there. It was vitally important for me to:

- Listen to the Holy Spirit as He revealed truth to me.
- Be open to the Holy Spirit's direction, conviction and counsel after He had my attention.
- Be willing to line up my life next to the Word of God.
- Permit others to help identify deception in my life.
- Be willing to make changes when I knew my life was not lining up with the Word.
- Have caring accountability partners.

VARIOUS HINDRANCES

There will always be hindrances to the work of the Holy Spirit. Some of those hindrances involve people. When we live in fear of others we are in bondage to them. When we are addicted to others opinions of us, we are slaves to their words. When we hold a grudge against someone, we are in bondage to them. Satan loves nothing more than for us to be in bondage to each other. To help break that bondage to those who have hurt us, we must learn a simple truth:

When we develop compassion and pity for those who have hurt us, we find we are able to be healed.

When others hurt us, generally the last thing we desire is to feel compassion for them. Our sense of fairness and damaged emotions tell us they deserve to be hurt in return. They deserve feeling our justifiable anger. They deserve our wrath and vengeance. They need to be hurt like they have hurt us.

We seem to live in a society that seems intent on blame. We hear much about litigation, punitive damages and wrongful hurt. We read and hear of outlandish settlements for wounds that are real or hurts that are only perceived. Our intellect and emotional mind can simply overwhelm our spiritual mind as we seek out vengeance and revenge.

When we realistically look at the situation and the person who hurt us, many times the wrongdoer does not even know they have hurt us. They are going on with their lives with no regrets or knowledge. Sometimes they do know, but simply do not care. In either case, we become the one in bondage. The hurt can rule our days and ruin our nights. We gnash our teeth in despair and anguish over the unresolved and non-avenged hurt. We simply cannot get over it, under it, or around it. We demand restitution. We demand justice. We demand an apology before we can move on. When the justice does not come, our hurt goes deeper and deeper.

35

HOW DEEP IS OUR HURT?

The higher altitude mountain peaks around the world have what are called "stations" for mountain climbers. Those stations are points on the progression up the mountain where there is a resting spot and staging area for the next step. As the new explorers get to the higher elevations and the upper stations, they see some of the remnants of earlier expeditions.

The consequences of hurt are like a six station mountain. The flat land at the base of the mountain is life. It is the place where we experience everyday living as we know it. This is where the journey begins.

Station #1 - Hurt

In that flatland area called life, we experience many things. However, as we have discussed earlier, one of the realities of life is something we call hurt. *Hurt* is Station 1 in the foothills of the mountain peaks. Hurt occurs when someone:

- Hurts our feelings
- Ignores us
- Gossips about us
- Does not show us respect
- Embarrasses us
- Reduces our ability to succeed
- Does not fulfill our expectations
- Says something hurtful to us
- Is abusive to us

These wounds can be real or imagined. They are hurtful in either case. These occurrences are a fact of life. They are things we experience in our homes, among our families, at our work, in our churches and in the fast food lines. If we are unable to dismiss these hurts, we move to the next station.

Station #2 - Anger

If we did not deal with the hurt in the foothills, we begin our gradual trek to Station 2, called *anger*. All of us know about this station. It is low enough on the mountain that we have made the journey here before. We recognize the symptoms of this emotion by:

- The feeling in the pit of our stomach
- The sweaty palms
- An accelerated heart rate
- The desire to strike back
- Our quick and sharp words
- Our defensiveness
- Loss of appetite or an out of control appetite
- Loss of sleep
- Loss of enjoyment in life

Anger defines the emotion which rises quickly and brings about actions that we later wish we would have controlled. Hurt is the instrument that caused the wound, while anger is the white-hot pain in the wound. It brings an intensity that demands something be done.

Station #3 - Resentment

If we do not deal with hurt and anger, we move up to Station 3, called *resentment*. Even though we have experienced this emotion, it is a bit more difficult to define.

We recognize resentment as the emotion that stops us from having fellowship or a relationship with someone. When you add the following feelings to hurt and anger, the result is resentment.

- We simply would rather not be around that person.
- A wall is beginning to be built between us.

37

- We are disturbed by their success.
- We are disturbed by happiness in their life.
- We go out of our way to distance ourselves from them.
- We desire to tell others about their transgression.

The emotions we felt with anger are still present with resentment. When this resentment occurs between a husband and wife, one or both may use the silent treatment. It is the time when tenderness, compassion, mercy, kind words, compliments or intimacy is withheld from the other spouse.

Resentment is the ongoing memory of the hurt and the deep wound. The memory brings back the pain and the knowledge that the object of hurt was not dealt with. Resentment is ongoing anger.

Station #4 - Bitterness

As we trudge our way to Station 4 we find a signpost called *bitterness.* The emotions of hurt, anger and resentment are still with us. Did you notice how the emotions began to compound and multiply as we moved up the steep incline? We can begin to comprehend the weight and heaviness of this baggage. It has multiplied when the emotions of the original hurt, anger and resentment are added to bitterness. It becomes a load nearly too heavy to carry. At this point:

- We begin to do things which are hurtful to the person who hurt us.
- We say or do things to get revenge.
- Our comments to them are sharp and damaging.
- Our physical and emotional actions and inactions can be negative.
- We gossip about them for the purpose of turning others against them.
- We may do or say things to damage their reputation.

- We plot ways to bring failure or hurt to their life.

When bitterness enters into a marriage, we soon see the devastation. The physical, mental and or verbal abuse may start at this stage. The Word cautions us about bitterness:

Colossians 3:19: Husbands, love your wives, and be not bitter against them.

Without resolution, bitterness escalates to a point where other individuals are drawn in and hurt. Again, God identifies the consequences:

Hebrews 12:15: Looking diligently lest any man fail of the grace of God; lest any root of bitterness springing up trouble you, and thereby many be defiled.

Bitterness is multiplied resentment. It is more than the sum of all of the hurts, anger and resentment brought about by someone over a period of time. Or, it may simply be the result of one issue or occurrence that has been allowed to fester. Bitterness may be directed towards a person, God, an institution, a group of people or an object.

Station #5 - Hatred

When we do not stop this devastating progression, the sequence moves us on to Station 5. This station has a very ugly and repulsive billboard called *hatred*. It is no longer a signpost, but rather a billboard. It is large and easily visible for all to see.

All of the earlier emotions of hurt, anger, resentment and bitterness are still present. When we progress to hatred, we begin to self-destruct. When we have hatred within us, we are quickly identified by those around us. There are many words and statements which can describe us.

- We are conniving, scheming, cunning and shrewd.
- We are deceitful and untrustworthy.
- We are focused on vengeance and revenge.
- We are devious and underhanded.
- We are angry, resentful and bitter.
- We are venomous and malicious.
- All that was good within us has either already disappeared or is nearly gone.
- We wish death and eternal destruction upon those who have hurt us.
- Our face soon physically shows what is internalized within us.
- Our physical, mental and emotional health deteriorates.

Hatred is an emotion and sin that carries with it immense amounts of consequences. Sad are the people who find themselves the victim of a hateful person.

The distance between this station of hate and the next station is short. Hatred tends to bring horrible consequences to both the hated and the hater. The accumulated baggage of hurt, anger, resentment and bitterness is now unbearably heavy.

Station #6 - Destruction

Station 6 is the summit. There is nothing beyond. It is the end of the trail. The hateful and vengeful people now take things into their own hands. Sadly, some of us reach this station known as <u>destruction</u>. All of the earlier emotions have taken their toll. The only thing left is either destroying the person who has hurt us or destroying ourselves.

We see the results of this played out in the world every day. We read of it, hear of it, and witness it ourselves. It is evident in a multitude of ways. These addictive behaviors are forms of self-destruction.

- Drug abuse
- Alcohol abuse
- Promiscuous sex
- Pornography
- Some obsessions

Destruction occurs in other ways:

- Self-mutilation
- Suicide
- Murder
- Rape
- Terrorism
- Violence

GOD'S PLAN

God has a much better plan, which brings abundant life and peace. It is difficult to feel a God given peace or inner joy when we have anger, resentment, bitterness or hatred towards someone. The concept of developing compassion for someone who has hurt us is the beginning of forgiveness. It is the beginning of moving beyond the past where possibly we have been mired for too long. Are we mired? Are we caught in the web? Has our joy and peace been replaced with anger and resentment? If so, there is hope. It begins with seeing ourselves for who we are.

IS MY WOUND HEALING?

It is important to remember that healing is a process. It does not happen overnight. Do not get discouraged when you cannot sense the progress. Progress is slow and arduous.

If your stopover at the bitterness station is only 1 day instead of your typical 5 days, you are making progress. If you stopped at anger and never got to your usual resentment station you are making progress.

It reminds me of a time when we were observing someone climbing the face of a vertical mountain cliff. The cliff face was what appeared to be a sheer wall of granite several hundred feet tall. The climber was a speck on the side of the cliff. He had no ropes. His advancement was imperceptible to the naked eye. Through binoculars we could view his progress: one arm at a time; one leg at a time; one handhold in a tiny crevice; a toe hold on a protrusion he could only feel and not see. I was excited to see him move towards his goal. I wanted to yell out to him, "Hang in there, you're getting close", but he would not be able to hear me. He could not see the top of the cliff. *He* did not know how much further *he* had to go, but *I* knew he was making progress and was getting increasingly closer.

Progress in the journey of healing is likewise slow and arduous. We can feel as alone as the climber on the rock face. We are not always able to recognize progress or see the goal. We should never give up. There are those on the sidelines who can assure us of progress. Surround yourself with encouragers. Believe them when they tell you of your progress.

> One of the most difficult things in life is to see ourselves clearly. Are we among the select group which is in need of healing? Are there areas of our lives which need to be dealt with? The next chapter will assist in answering those questions.

- 3 -

AM I A BAGGAGE CARRIER?

Several years ago, my son, Rick, and I backpacked the Western area of the Grand Canyon. We each carried a 40-pound pack loaded with the essentials we needed to get through several days in the Canyon. Our goal was to get to the Havasupai Indian Reservation and beyond, spend a couple of days there and return.

When it came time to hike out of the Canyon, we made a decision. We paid a man from the Havasupai Indian Reservation to take our packs out by pack horse. Instead of carrying our 40-pound packs, Rick and I each carried about 10 pounds of essentials. Without the extra baggage, we saw and experienced much more than we did on the way in. We were able to hike some side canyons and see things we never would have seen if we would have carried the extra weight. We were free and unencumbered! The trip up the trail to the rim was bearable and much more enjoyable.

As we begin this journey of learning how to deal with hurt, it is necessary for us to determine if we are carrying emotional baggage. Are there hurts we still feel or issues we remember? We gather emotional baggage in a variety of ways beginning with our earliest memories. We pick up emotional baggage from strangers as well as those to whom we are close.

Do you recall one of the questions we are asked when we check in at an airport ticket counter?

*"Has anyone asked you to carry something
for them on this flight?"*

45

I have never been in a situation where someone has asked me to carry something for them on a flight. However, I do know about people giving me emotional things to carry. Following are some illustrations that will help you determine whether or not you are weighted down with baggage.

Most of our earliest memories begin at possibly three years of age. However, some of our baggage begins right after birth.

EARLY PROGRAMMING

When I became self-employed several years ago, I knew I would need a new computer system. I considered three options. First, I could purchase a used system for a significantly reduced price. Secondly, I could buy a new retail system off the shelf at a computer outlet for an economical price. Thirdly, I could have a computer outlet build a custom computer per my specifications. The used option and the standard retail option were attractive because of their reduced price. However, they both had the same liability. I would have to use what someone else thought was necessary or what they thought I needed. I desired something that would fit my needs. I had specific needs for a word processor, Scripture software, a financial package and an Internet ready system. So, I made the decision to spend the extra money and have a computer built specifically for my needs. When I brought it home and plugged it in, the computer was just what I desired and what I had designed it to be.

On September 8, 1973, our daughter, Tonia, was born. She was a beautiful little package created in Heaven and delivered directly to Jeni and me. I can see some similarities between Tonia and my new custom built computer system that was built specifically for me.

God gave us a very unique and special package when He gave us Tonia. God had placed some standard things within her, such as being female, a particular personality, hair and eye color.

46

The list goes on and on. However, beginning the day she was born, some of her options began to be programmed.

The programming was accomplished over a course of years by a group of programming experts. Jeni and I as her parents, her brother Rick, grandpas, grandmas, aunts, uncles, Sunday School teachers, public school teachers, friends and strangers. Even now, with a husband and four children, her programming continues. She has become a unique person partly due to tremendous amounts of input, as is true with each of us.

We are able to retain much of the input that has found its way into our minds and lives. We have many wonderful memories of the things that have formed us and shaped us. We remember the warm and fuzzy feelings that came with having puppies and kittens that taught us how to love. We remember feeling special at birthday parties and the great memories of Christmas gatherings with families and friends. We remember uncles and aunts who went out of their way to teach us basic truths about life. We think of uncles who took us fishing and grandpas who always had a pocketful of candy. Our lives reflect the positive memories and influences those good times have had on us.

EARLY BAGGAGE
In spite of all the good experiences that formed us, we were also shaped by the negative and detrimental things. As children we were affected and programmed by many subtle as well as not-so-subtle influences.

- A father who is absent
- A demanding mother
- A parent who cannot show tenderness
- A parent unable to convey compassion or mercy
- A parent who cannot express outward expressions of affection
- Merciless teasing from a relative

47

- A little child who has been humiliated or scolded in front of their friends
- A child who is physically, emotionally, verbally or sexually abused

Obviously, the programming comes from many sources in many ways. As children we begin to wear our background and experiences like a child who wears a Halloween costume. We become something different from what we were created to be. We become something different than what is outwardly apparent. What is external is a distortion of what may be under the surface.

Those early experiences and programming make us different and unique within the ocean of humanity.

DIFFERENCES ARE GOOD?

Throughout life, we are exposed to many different people with diverse differences. As people, we are very unique individuals and unfortunately, differences can and do bring conflict. Those differences also enrich our lives and stretch us far beyond our comfort zones. We dare not forget the old saying:

"You do not get harmony when everyone sings the same note."

God created uniqueness and differences to add richness and abundance to our lives. It is not His goal to have those differences create conflicts. However, reality has taught us differences can and do bring conflict. It is important for us to minimize the conflicts, but not to minimize the differences. Once the differences are understood, the conflicts are reduced, minimized or simply disappear.

We learn quickly that life has its idealism as well as its reality. Over the course of time, negative input from others may become perceived truth for us when, in actuality, it is deception. When a young child receives input, his ability to sort out truth from deception is minimal. Therefore, a young child takes in data and processes it as truth only to find out later as an adult they have been deceived. It is vitally important for us to identify some of the deception in our lives we have come to accept as truth.

Our Heavenly Father has a great desire that we would know truth in every aspect of our lives. Deception robs Believers and nonbelievers alike, of the very best God has to offer His creation. A very important Scripture for us is found in the Gospel of John:

John 8:32: And ye shall know the truth, and the truth shall make you free.

As the Holy Spirit reveals truth to us, we learn how to cope with the cold and hard realities of life. Then, we can seek to unravel some of the deception taught to us by society and people in general. God's desire for each of us is to be in His image and in His likeness. It is His desire that we would be Spirit-filled, Christ-like and Godly. A difficult task indeed, when we are struggling with hurt feelings, anger, rejection, failure, defensiveness, bitterness and hatred. The Holy Spirit can show us the areas of our lives which need to be reclaimed.

ARE WE AMONG THE DECEIVED?

I have been in some exquisite caverns in my lifetime. The beauty of the stalactites and stalagmites, the glittering of the crystals, the blackness of the "lights out" time, and the chill of the air were wonderful parts of the tours through those caverns. Then there are the natural caverns of southern Indiana that have not been "cleaned" from the mud and dirt of centuries past. Those caves are capable of being explored, but the journey is not one of beauty. The trek into the depths of our emotions is not very inviting either. Nevertheless, it is rewarded by freedom from some bondage issues of life.

My own emotional and spiritual trek took me into some ugly areas, such as bitterness and hatred. I was amazed at what I discovered in my emotional past. Memories and feelings had been in my mind and heart, though they were covered by many years of denial, defensiveness and justification. They had been lurking somewhere in the dark recesses of my mind, forgotten by choice or simply for survival.

Counselors are sometimes asked: "As a converted, born-again Believer, is it scriptural for me to dig into the past after my old and sinful life has been cleansed? If I am a new creature in Christ and the old has passed away (2 Corinthians 5:17), do I have the right or the authority to look back?" Let us consider:

2 Corinthians 7:1: Having therefore these promises, dearly beloved, let us cleanse ourselves from all filthiness of the flesh and spirit, perfecting holiness in the fear of God.

If we desire to be Godly, Christ-like and Spirit-filled, we must walk daily with Him. Unresolved issues from our past can interfere with this walk. Is it realistic to believe there may be things from our past that need attention? It is God's desire that each of His children would not be hindered in living the abundant life:

John 10:10: The thief cometh not, but for to steal, and to kill, and to destroy: I am come that they might have life, and that they might have it more abundantly.

Luke 12:32: Fear not, little flock; for it is your Father's good pleasure to give you the kingdom.

He does not give up in bringing the abundant life to us. Many years ago, He permitted me to hear two sermons with a very specific message. That specific message simply would not leave my mind. Those sermons were the inauguration of a new beginning for me. I was led to my past just as surely as a horse is led to water.

HOW ABOUT YOU?
We can ask ourselves a variety of questions to determine if we have some of the symptoms of "emotional hurt" and are carrying baggage:

- Do you experience hurt feelings?
- Do you get defensive when you are challenged?
- Do you consider yourself as having "narrow" shoulders?
- Are you too sensitive?
- Do you have thin skin?
- Do others need to walk around you with care?
- Do you find yourself getting angry about small and trivial issues?
- Are you an impatient person?
- Do you carry grudges from yesterday or the past?
- Is the love you give or receive conditional?
- Is it difficult for you to have close relationships with others?
- Does God seem distant?
- Does God seem harsh and judgmental?
- Is it difficult for you to say you are sorry?
- Is it tough to feel compassion and pity for those who wrong you?
- Is forgiving those who hurt you difficult?
- Have you ever experienced the abundant life?
- Do you have feelings of shame about your past?
- Do you feel like others are to blame for your mistakes?

- Is it difficult for you to accept compliments?
- Is it hard for you to believe you have spiritual gifts?
- Do you feel you have no "worth"?

"Yes" answers to these questions may be an indication of emotional baggage and unresolved hurt. Answering the above questions honestly is the first step to healing your emotionally troubled past. It is difficult or impossible to help people who think they have no problems. Do you have some hurt waiting to be healed? Are you a baggage carrier?

We have explored how we are molded and shaped by our very early life experiences as well as our ongoing life experiences. Some of those personal and relational experiences bring emotional baggage.

However, not all of our baggage comes from the programming carried out by those around us. Unfortunately, some of our baggage may come from misinterpretations of the Bible. In the next chapter, we will define how this can occur.

54

- 4 -

IDEALISM OF THE BIBLE

FALSE GUILT

A woman told me recently she feels immense guilt and condemnation when she hears a sermon about loving God with *all* her heart, soul, mind and strength. When she hears this message, she loses all hope of ever being a "good" Christian. She thinks she has never measured up to this standard, nor did she think she ever would. In her mind she has already failed, so why try?

We are taught to believe the Bible is the inspired and infallible Word of God. God's holiness requires adherence to the principles and doctrines of His Word. As Christians, we sometimes struggle with meeting the ideals found in the Bible.

In this chapter, I do not intend to expound on God's standards for us as Christians, but rather seek to explain the balance between His justice *and* His grace. Greater joy comes to those who more fully understand His standards *and* His mercy.

Let us take a look at some of the Scripture phrases and words which may bring us guilt.

Mark 12:30: And thou shalt love the Lord thy God with all thy heart, and with all thy soul, and with all thy mind, and with all thy strength...

1 Peter 1:16: Because it is written, Be ye holy; for I am holy...

Matthew 5:48: Be ye therefore perfect, even as your Father which is in heaven is perfect.

1 John 5:18: We know that whosoever is born of God sinneth not; but he that is begotten of God keepeth himself, and that wicked one toucheth him not.

BALANCE

Too much emphasis on God's justice can result in fear, lack of the abundant life and a questioning of our salvation. Too much emphasis on His grace, mercy and love can cause us to be lukewarm, backslide or have an indifference to sin. God desires to help us find balance, and thus the abundant life by our use of the Bible and the power of His Holy Spirit.

The epistles are full of precepts and doctrines for our Christian walk. The reality of living on planet Earth can be troublesome for Christians who are seeking to live up to the standards of the Word. Learning more about these principles helps us better understand our Father's heart.

As we search the New Testament, we observe the harsh realities of life lived out in the lives of Paul, Peter, Ananias and Sapphira, Judas, Matthew, John and many others. We read about the struggles between Paul and Barnabas. We read about persecutions, but we also see the sufficiency of God's grace in every situation. Paul knew hurt, trouble, sorrow, disappointment, discouragement, failure and rejection throughout his converted life. We get a glimpse of Paul's day to day reality in:

2 Corinthians 11:24-28: Of the Jews five times received I forty stripes save one. [25] Thrice was I beaten with rods, once was I stoned, thrice I suffered shipwreck, a night and a day I have been in the deep; [26] In journeyings often, in perils of waters, in perils of robbers, in perils by mine own countrymen, in perils by the heathen, in perils in the city, in perils in the wilderness, in perils

in the sea, in perils among false brethren; [27] In weariness and painfulness, in watchings often, in hunger and thirst, in fastings often, in cold and nakedness. [28] Beside those things that are without, that which cometh upon me daily, the care of all the churches.

Paul's life was just as real as ours. His relationships with people were much like ours. He knew the harsh realities of life.

Our lives likewise are filled with real situations and real people. We live in a society which is becoming more and more self-centered. We have to deal with issues such as abortion, terrorism, and other situations that are anti-Christ and anti-family. Learning how to cope in a sinful world is a necessity for a converted, born-again Believer.

Our measure of joy and our abundant life is in direct proportion to how well we learn to cope with the hurts and the imperfections which surround us. We constantly see imperfections in ourselves, in those we love as well as in complete strangers. We live in an imperfect society, world and universe.

But God understands...

Psalms 103:14: For he knoweth our frame; he remembereth that we are dust.

Because He understands, He has provided a way for us to overcome...

John 3:16: For God so loved the world, that he gave his only begotten Son, that whosoever believeth in him should not perish, but have everlasting life.

The death, shed blood and subsequent resurrection of God's perfect sacrifice, Jesus Christ, give us hope and a promise of eternal life in Heaven. God calls us to have faith in the shed blood and give our lives to Him. He calls us to repent, be converted and born-again. In return, God helps us cope by giving us His grace. By His grace and with our living faith, He forgives the differences He sees between the ideals expressed in Scripture and the harsh realities of our lives.

By knowing God's great desire for us to go to Heaven, we are better able to understand the Scriptures...

Ezekiel 33:11: Say unto them, As I live, saith the Lord God, I have no pleasure in the death of the wicked.

1 Tim. 2:4: (God) Who will have all men to be saved, and to come unto the knowledge of the truth.

Luke 12:32: Fear not, little flock; for it is your Father's good pleasure to give you the kingdom.

GUILT

In the Bible, the emotion of guilt is associated with sin and judgment. Satan is the great master and manipulator of this emotion and concept. Many Christians today feel guilty for their thoughts, feelings, remarks and actions. Satan uses this to cause a born-again Believer to be spiritually handicapped. He knows guilt can make us inactive and ineffective in God's vineyard. It is important for us to have a clear understanding of this emotion called "guilt". Are we experiencing false guilt from satan or do we feel true conviction from the Holy Spirit?

Unless we understand this concept, it is difficult to break satan's power over us. We will continue to feel we cannot change or even improve. We will be overwhelmed by a face-in-the-dirt kind of helplessness.

Can we understand the difference? Here are a few questions to think about when we are feeling overwhelmed with failure:

1. Do I feel like I am condemned forever?
2. Do I feel hopelessly entangled in the situation?
3. Do I feel unable to change or improve?
4. Do I see any possible good coming from this situation?

If we listen to satan when we fail, we feel condemned and hopeless. We do not see a way out of the problem and we can not imagine God ever bringing good out of the situation. In our hopelessness, we think life will never be any different. We feel we will never be able to change.

Guilt is a de-motivator for Godly living. In fact, guilt feeds an attitude that we have failed so often, we may as well give up trying. What could be the end result of utter hopelessness? Possibly hopelessness would lead to self-destruction.

If satan can get us to believe our feelings come from God, then he has succeeded in accomplishing his task of deceiving us. It is essential we know and understand God's heart so we can know the difference between conviction and false guilt. If we do not learn that difference, we will not understand God's motives. We will blame God for hurts which come our way and we will never get past asking "Why?"

One of the verses in the Bible that most clearly illustrates the desire of God and the motivations of satan is:

John 10:10: The thief cometh not, but for to steal, and to kill, and to destroy: I am come that they might have life, and that they might have it more abundantly.

In the corporate world, we have job descriptions. John 10:10 lays out the job description of satan and the beauty of our Lord. Let us look at them side by side:

satan	God
to steal	to give life
to kill	to bring the abundant life
to destroy	

As we look at the previous paragraphs again, it becomes very clear as to where condemnation and hopelessness come from. We must never forget the clear message of hope, love and mercy which God gives to Believers through the life, death, blood and resurrection of Jesus.

Following are some of the feelings or thoughts we may experience if we have false guilt:

- You should read and study the Bible more.
- Your prayers should be much more sincere.
- You should spend more time visiting the widows and orphans.
- You should love the Lord with all your heart, mind and strength.
- You should have more zeal for the unconverted.
- You should give more money to the poor.

Aside from the accusing and condemning attitude of the statements, each of the accusations has a common word - should. Many times we can recognize satan's presence by the guilt-producing words we use or hear in our thoughts, such as; should, should have, could, could have, would, would have, ought and ought to have. His accusations cause us to have feelings of hopelessness, shame and guilt.

Are those words in our vocabulary? If you think they may be, ask someone close to you to monitor your comments and tell you if they are hearing them.

CONVICTION

Let us take a look at the conviction of the Holy Spirit. The Bible tells us in:

Romans 8:14 - For as many as are led by the Spirit of God, they are the sons of God.

When we receive the Holy Spirit, we are led by God. The conviction of His Spirit works in us in a manner 180 degrees opposite from the condemning guilt of satan.

The Holy Spirit's conviction is a gift from God. It has great power. The Holy Spirit gives us the knowledge of our transgression, plus the ability to change.

When we have done something wrong, the Spirit quietly influences our souls with a gentle tugging which brings conviction. This is what is referred to as the "still small voice" of God. Along with this conviction, we experience God's hope and grace.

The presence of this hope is the most distinguishing difference between satan's guilt and the Holy Spirit's conviction.

MY EXPERIENCE

For years, I would give satan the time or ear he desired. Without thinking, I would debate and argue with him in my mind whenever he would indict me with any of his accusatory statements. He would continually accuse me of my failings.

Then something occurred to me... I began to think about the awesome power of my Father God. I realized my prayers would never be sincere enough to pay the debt which I owed Him. I realized I could never work hard enough to pay back the huge price Jesus paid for my soul. It was at that point I realized satan's accusations were true. I could never argue with satan about truth. It was a losing battle. My works would never be sufficient enough to merit God's blessings.

With this new mind set, satan's accusations lost their power. The Lord Jesus Himself gave me the answer in dealing with satan:

Luke 4:8: And Jesus answered and said unto him; Get thee behind me, Satan.

OUR RESPONSIBILITY

Thus we are able to respond to satan's accusations as Jesus did, with the command, "Get behind me, satan".

Our Father is not asking us for perfection. Our Father is asking us to do the best we can by His power and by His grace. Our Father is asking us to never forget the blood and life which Jesus paid for our souls. The Holy Spirit can become stronger, more meaningful and more apparent in our lives when we are able to quiet the boisterous, accusatory and arrogant voice of satan.

The Holy Spirit will then be able to convict us in new ways.

I am always amazed at the ingenious ways which God's Holy Spirit can convict us and encourage us!

- While talking to a newly converted person who is zealous for God's Word, we may hear the still small voice of the Holy Spirit convicting us to study the Bible more often and with more fervor.
- When we see a small child in tattered clothing we may be touched and pricked to action.
- If we have a difficult situation at home or work, we can literally be driven to prayer and the Word for answers.

- A sermon can bring new truth to our ears. This may touch our hearts and bring conviction.
- Seeing someone homeless may prompt us to positive action.
- The sadness of an orphan may move us to tears and may inspire us to provide financial support.
- When we read or hear about persecuted Christians around the world, we may be prompted to regularly pray for them and seek ways in which to help relieve their suffering.

THE FATHER'S LOVE

The Lord knows love and tenderness will produce greater results than punishing accusations. I learned that lesson well on the knees of my dad in 1959. I was 10 years old and had just lied to him. I was caught because God had given Dad the evidence he needed. Dad invited me into the bathroom for one of those daddy-to-son talks. My dad believed in literally applying the verse in Proverbs:

Proverbs 22:15: Foolishness is bound in the heart of a child; but the *rod of correction* shall drive it far from him.

As I bent over his knees preparing for the inevitable, I looked up into his eyes and saw tears welling up and starting to flow down his cheeks. Observing his compassion and love for me taught me much about the difference between loving-discipline and unloving-punishment.

Satan tries to get us to do wrong things, but he is content to see us do the right thing for the wrong reason. Doing the right thing for the wrong reason promotes "religion". Doing the right thing for the right reason promotes spirituality. Since my dad was doing the right thing for the right reason his loving discipline deepened my love for him and increased my desire to be good.

RESULTS OF THE FATHER'S LOVE

Many times, we act or react negatively or wrongly because of hurts. If we <u>truly</u> understood what God thinks of us and how much He loves us, do you think we would still act and react in a negative way? Would other people be able to make us angry so quickly or hurt us so deeply if we had a deeper relationship with God? If our relationship with God could grow, would the opinions of others mean nearly as much to us?

Having a better understanding about the heart of God can deepen our love for Him. Seeing Him more clearly can promote our devotion to Him. Seeing ourselves more clearly can teach us the truth about our unrighteousness and can make us realize our need for His righteousness. We must believe in the idealism of the Scripture, yet we must believe the absolute futility of our own efforts. We should never doubt His deep love for us. Let us keep in mind:

Philip. 4:13: I can do all things through Christ which strengtheneth me.

When we begin to understand His righteousness, His love, as well as the weakness of our human flesh, we can begin to comprehend how patient He is. Since He grants mercy to us on a regular basis, we must grant mercy to others. For us to be able to grant that mercy to others, we need to understand how and why we are different from one another.

It is important to remember God's love for us. It is important to know and embrace Biblical truth so we do not have misconceptions about God and His Word. The next chapter should help us better understand our relationship with God and His Word. When we are able to know Him more fully, we will not be as likely to misunderstand His motives and priorities. Then we will be able to think of Him as a loving Father and be able to return His love more deeply.

What does God think about His creation? Is He blessed by us? What is the motivation behind His love of us? Does He love us unconditionally? The next chapter explores who we are in God's eyes.

- 5 -

WHAT IS MAN?

In a group session I was in recently, young women were talking about their relationships with their fathers as they grew up. One talked about her dad working so many hours that she rarely saw him. Another mentioned she had never heard anything encouraging or positive from her father. Then, the room grew quiet as another young lady talked of her experiences with her dad. She said it was a rare day when her father did not tell her she was beautiful and sweet. When she came home from school, her dad would ask her about her day. He made her feel very special, secure and unconditionally loved. She really believed she had worth. I could literally see the expressions of envy on the faces of the other women.

This chapter deals with the relationships between us and our Heavenly father. When we are able to clearly see how much God loves us and how much He desires to bless us, our perception of ourselves can improve dramatically. Then, when someone hurts us, we are able to realize we still have worth in God's eyes. We find He is there to help pick up the pieces of our broken lives and mend the fences between people. It is important for us to understand more completely what God sees when He looks at us.

SEEING GOD

Early one Sunday morning, I decided to take a half-mile walk down a country lane to a pond. I was looking for a 20-minute respite from the rest of the world. While walking, I noticed a glistening shimmer on the grass ahead of me. As I got closer, I could see the shimmer was actually a 12-inch diameter spider web, covered with dew and catching the early rays of the sun. As I knelt beside it, I was filled with awe at the intricacies of the web. It was then I noticed the web, though flat had a tunnel spiraling down into the grass. As I peered into the tunnel, I could see the home of the spider. I continued on my walk, and observed there were 20 or 30 more of those webs ahead, each having its own tunnel. They were magnificent!

I got to the pond and sat on the pier. The water was clear, and so still there was hardly a ripple. I looked over the edge of the pier and noticed a small glistening speck about the size of a pencil lead. Then I saw several more. Suddenly a water bug about the size of a fly, hydro foiled towards the speck! As the bug approached and bumped into the spot, the spot jumped an inch into the air and an inch away from the waterbug. I was flabbergasted a spot that tiny could jump! The world around me stopped momentarily as I observed the marvel taking place before me. Life and death was unfolding in front of me! The chase ensued within a square foot arena until the living speck disappeared into what it must have perceived as the cavernous jaws of that tiny water bug. I watched enthralled as more water bugs and more spots jumped until they became breakfast.

It was then I heard a splash and saw the flash of a bluegill sunfish jumping in the sunlight, as a water bug became his breakfast. I wondered about the cycle of life. I was in awe at how God takes care of all His creation.

The ripples of that splashing bluegill started to spread over the pond. The ripples just kept going and going and going...

Deciding to head home, I noticed a 3-inch limestone rock full of bumps. I picked it up and brushed the dust from it. It was a piece of limestone which had serrations of some very early shell. I marveled at the wonder of it all.

Walking another 50 feet, I noticed the most magnificent blue wildflower. It was so gorgeously blue! It was a deep blue that would have rivaled the most magnificent Caribbean depths. There were 14 tiny petals that were so delicate and soft.

I looked at my watch. My 20-minute walk had turned into a 45-minute journey into God's country. While I was watching how God takes care of the birds, fish, bugs, and flowers of His fields, I realized how He had just taken care of and refreshed me in a miraculous way. I had been blessed, intrigued and fascinated by His little things. Is it any wonder that at the end of each creation day, God saw that it was good?

WHAT A WEEK!

We have a marvelous portion of Scripture that describes creation in a beautiful way. Genesis Chapter 1 depicts a wonderful beginning for planet Earth and its inhabitants. As the creation unfolded in those early days, the world became increasingly more beautiful, more complete and more magnificent. Each day progressively built upon the day before. Each new dawning of day revealed yet more beauty rivaling the beauty of the day before.

Through our human senses, we can experience the glory and majesty of His creation.

- We see His grandeur at the Grand Canyon, the Alps, and the East African Serengeti Plains filled with zebra, giraffe, antelope, lions and kudu.
- We stand in awe as we see and hear the power of Niagara Falls.
- We witness the endless tides of the oceans.
- We are touched by the powerful majesty of the great Killer Whales.
- Our mind cannot comprehend the tiny, endless fluttering of a hummingbird drinking the nectar of soft-petaled glorious and colorful flowers.

- Our innermost being is terrorized by the ferocious roar of a lion.
- Our innermost being is touched by the tiny meow of a little kitten.
- Our sense of touch is amazed at the soft whiskers of a baby kitten.
- Our mind is overwhelmed at the trust and love of a puppy for his master.
- Our eyes are mysteriously mesmerized by the iridescence and luminance of a jellyfish.
- Our high intelligence is blindsided by the untold and profound mysteries of DNA.
- Our memories are immersed with every sunset and every sunrise we have seen.
- Our eyes and our minds simply cannot fathom the endless reaches of an eternal universe.
- The largest computers cannot tabulate the brilliance or numbers of zillions of stars.
- The largest scales in the world cannot maintain the balance of the planets.
- Scientists are astounded at the predictability of a comet.
- We are always searching for identical snowflakes as we contemplate the intricacy and individuality of each snowflake.

The Lord God created it all, and at the end of every day, the Bible states the same thing, "and God saw that it was _good_!"

Every day we can witness the magnificence of His creation. We read again and again in Genesis of the beginnings of it all. In spite of the repetition, we are still captivated by His majesty. Though we see His beauty from the smallest elements of creation to the vast depths and heights of the universe, we read in the Bible what He created to be His crowning glory.

It is _man_!

Genesis 1:26: And God said, Let us make man in our image, after our likeness.

Then because man had a living soul and was created in the image and likeness of God, we have:

Genesis 1:31: And God saw _every_ thing that he had made, and, behold, it was _very good_...

IMPERFECT MAN WAS HIS CROWNING GLORY ?
In our finite humanness, it is difficult for us to comprehend that the creation of one man took the glorious splendor of the newly created universe from the status of "good" to "very good." But, this is the scriptural truth of God's view of man. His view of man was not due to the achievements of Adam. God chose then, and continues to choose now, to view man as His crowning glory.

Unfortunately, we only need to turn a page of the Bible to see how quickly man gave up that revered position. Man's immorality, corruption and depravity became apparent very quickly. We learn about the lives of Cain and Abel, as well as the evil generations of men and women and the great flood. We see how our lives can be different today, and yet, we still deal with the depravity of man.

However, God has already dealt with this depravity. His justice and His Word ordain the future of humanity. We have a hope, and a possibility of renewing our closeness with Him through the sacrifice of the perfect lamb, Jesus, the very Son of God. In the New Testament, we can learn about being born again, conversion, repentance and justification by faith. We can learn the concepts of holiness, sanctification, grace and the Holy Spirit. Then we can see the heart of God as we see the life of Jesus Christ unfolding. The Bible teaches us some very basic truths:

71

Romans 2:11: For there is no respect of persons with God.

Ezekiel 33:11: Say unto them, As I live, saith the Lord God, I have no pleasure in the death of the wicked.

1 Timothy 2:4: (God) who will have all men to be saved, and to come unto the knowledge of the truth.

1 John 4:16: ...God is love...

There can be no doubt about these scriptural truths:

1. God's desire is for all men to choose to serve Him.
2. God's desire is to have all men with Him in His eternal home called Heaven.
3. God is love. God is perfect. Therefore, His love is perfect.
4. He is not a "respecter of persons". Since He is love and it is a perfect love, He loves everyone to the same depth.
5. Perfect love is unconditional.
6. He hurts deeply when a soul chooses not to serve Him and not to accept His unconditional love and subsequent eternal home.

> When we view the life of a corrupt man versus the life of a man who desires the heart of God, our choice should be obvious. We know that realities of life guarantee we will be hurt by others on our journey. So, once again we move towards learning how to cope with those hurts when they occur. We will learn about eight coping mechanisms or skills in the upcoming chapters.

- 6 -

THE PROCESS OF COPING

Early in my ministry, I saw coping in action. A young couple in our congregation was on the receiving end of a tragedy. The father had been driving on a country road with his 3-year-old son. Another young lady failed to stop at a stop sign and broadsided the young father and his son. The little boy had his short life taken in an instant. I did not know the young lady, but because I knew she had to be going through a very difficult time, I went to visit her. She was experiencing horrendous guilt realizing she had caused an accident that had taken a life. The funeral for thc little boy was going to take place the next day. For her future welfare, I thought she should talk to the parents of the child. I knew the parent's hearts. I knew their faith. I knew it would be a beneficial experience for the guilt-ridden young lady.

The woman reluctantly agreed and went with me to the funeral home. When we got there, the grieving couple saw us coming, left the side of the casket, came over and wrapped their arms of love around this young woman. They comforted her in the midst of her grief and sobbing. I will never forget the scene as we witnessed the three of them intertwined. The sobbing woman was engrossed in such obvious guilt, shame and grief. The parents were tenderly sharing their love and giving comfort to the young lady. She was the recipient of their mercy, grace and love. Her life would never be the same because of the tragedy, as well as receiving the unconditional love of the parents whose

75

son's life had been taken. The wonderful love Jesus gives His people can soften even the harshest realities of life.

BIBLICAL COPING

The book of Job is excellent for us to read if we are to understand how to cope with the realities of life. Job had been hurt by his wife, by his friends, and for a time believed that God Himself was intent upon hurting him. It is very interesting, as we read through the chapters, to see how Job coped with life. By the time we reach the end of the book, it is clear Job had a very healthy perception of who God was and how God viewed him.

We likewise can read in the Bible about Joseph. We cannot fathom the hurt he must have felt in being betrayed, sold and separated from his family. In the last chapter of Genesis we read of the great fear Joseph's brothers had for their very lives:

Genesis 50:15: And when Joseph's brethren saw that their father was dead, they said, Joseph will peradventure hate us, and will certainly requite us all the evil which we did unto him.

But Joseph was filled with Godly understanding:

Genesis 50:19-20: And Joseph said unto them, Fear not: for am I in the place of God? [20] But as for you, ye thought evil against me; but God meant it unto good, to bring to pass, as it is this day, to save much people alive.

And then Joseph gave us a wonderful glimpse of unconditional love, mercy, compassion, grace and coping:

Genesis 50:21: Now therefore fear ye not: I will nourish you, and your little ones. And he comforted them, and spake kindly unto them.

76

Joseph had to know the abundant life. If he had not, he would not have been able to forgive those who had hurt him so deeply. He would not have been such a wonderful example of a peaceful and Godly man.

COPING IN THE 21st CENTURY

If we are to cope with the hurts which come our way, we need to learn the same concepts which Joseph had to learn. We need to understand what God sees when He looks at us. Likewise, we need to comprehend who God is. It is sometimes so difficult to get past the painful emotions caused by the hurt.

When we feel compassion, tenderness or pity for someone who has hurt us, the situation is fundamentally resolved. The key to this resolution is finding a reason to feel compassion towards the one who has hurt us. How can we do this when our emotions are crying out for vengeance? How can we do this when we are demanding justice for having been unjustly accused? It seems our lives afford us ample opportunities to find our way through the maze of forgiveness for those who are hurting us or have hurt us in the past.

There are ways for us to better understand the inappropriate actions, reactions or inactions of those who hurt us. Let us look at eight different types of coping mechanisms to help us better understand people. Let me state again, "It is the differences between us that cause us to react negatively to one another."

Someone shared with me recently how easily she is hurt by things her brother says to her. She has found it strange her nephew can say the same things to her and she can appreciate it coming from him. Why do we react so differently to different people? Why do some people naturally hurt our feelings or frustrate us?

77

OUR DIFFERENCES

The eight different areas we are exploring are applicable to each of us. These eight areas make us uniquely different from each other. In general, they are not things we have asked for, but rather they are qualities and characteristics which God has placed within us. Some of them are life experiences of which we had no control. They are things which make us all uniquely different and add flavor to our lives. When we understand this concept, it becomes easier to accept our differences.

The eight areas we will be looking at in the next chapters are:

- Gender – Male and Female
- Personality
- Backgrounds and Experiences
- Spiritual Gifts
- Fulfillment and Enrichment Factors
- The Emotionally Challenged
- Fears
- Love, Likes and Preferences

In each of the next chapters, we will look at specific illustrations to help us understand how learning to cope will benefit us.

Years ago, I could very easily turn a hurt into a grudge. That grudge could have lasted for years and affect my relationships with certain individuals.

Learning coping mechanisms does not necessarily take away the hurt. Those hurts become reality for us. Reality, as we explored in Chapter 1, is part of life. We will experience pain, and hurt will inevitably come. When we learn to *cope*, hurt does not need to last longer than two seconds, two minutes or two hours. The coping mechanisms can become so much a part of our lives, we rarely have to consciously think about them. The

78

process becomes automatic. We can learn to continually correct our faulty thinking. Doing this becomes a new way of living. It becomes a very redeeming life.

Now, let us move on to the eight areas which make each of us uniquely different in the ocean of humanity. We will investigate the areas that attract us to one another, as well as the differences which create hurt. Some topics will be more pertinent to us than others. However, as we begin to understand our differences, we will find ways which will help us grant mercy to others. The abundant life is coming.

> The differences between a male and female are many. We will seek to learn just how much they affect our everyday life in the next chapter.

HE CREATED THEM...
MALE AND FEMALE

Several years ago, Jeni and I were traveling from our home in Indiana to Illinois. The trip should have taken us five hours. We were scheduled to be at a dinner at someone's home at 5:00. The trip took us west on a major highway into a small town. A train was stopped on the railroad tracks blocking the highway. It looked like the train would be there awhile, so I decided to try a side street to find a way around the train.

(*Male Trait # 1* - If anything is in the way, find a way under it, over it or around it.)

I found a side street that took us through a park and into the country. I thought I was traveling west just as before so I stayed on that road rather than cutting back to the original and more heavily traveled highway. Knowing I was parallel to the original highway assured me I would reach my destination as expected.

(*Male Trait #2* - Use the inner compass God gives to every male for directions.)

Knowing I was traveling parallel to the earlier route, we drove for ten miles with virtually no traffic. I was feeling very smug and satisfied. What could possibly be wrong with that? I had found a faster, more convenient way of getting from point A to point B!

(*Male Trait #3* - When things are going good, do not change anything, just keep on keeping on.)

Jeni said, "Are you sure that we are going in the right direction?"

(*Male Trait #4* – God-given male trait #2 should never be questioned.)

 I said, "Absolutely. Of course," with an air of authority that began to seal my doom.

(*Male Trait #5* – Give a firm black and white answer to dispel any doubts or questions.)

She said, "Honey, I'm not sure about this road. There's a gas station, why don't you ask to make sure?"

(*Male Trait #6* – Do not back down even when you begin to feel doubt.)

I said, "Trust me," as my eyes casually and discreetly started to look for signs that would indicate I was in fact on the right road.

(*Lesson of Life #1* – Be careful how and when you say "*Trust me.*")

Seven miles later, I saw a sign for another town of which I was familiar. That town was almost 20 miles south of where I left the main road. I had been traveling straight south instead of west during my "short cut"! We were traveling away from the main road, not parallel to it. Can you imagine the difficulty of climbing out of this hole I created? So…

(*Male Trait #7* - Make an excuse.)

…I started in, "Darling, do you remember way back in Watseka when we went through that park? The roads in that little park were a bit curvy and not square with the world. That must have been the problem."

(*Male Trait #8* – Blame an inanimate object like a city park to eliminate self-blame.)

(*Female Trait #1* - Smile with an "I told you so" kind of smile.)

Results:
- Two gallons of gasoline wasted
- 40 miles out of the way
- 30 minutes late for dinner
- a very humbled husband
- a self-satisfied wife

OPPOSITES ATTRACT?

If we were all identical, it would seem hurts would be few and far between. Our similarities seem to be positives attracting us to one another. Our differences seem to divide and create hurt. There is an old saying which states "opposites attract." I believe that to be true for the short term, but over the long haul, our differences tend to create friction. Our differences create problems because of our sin nature.

In my opinion, those who hurt us most quickly and deeply are those who are most different from us. If we better understand the things that make us different from one another, we will more easily deal with the hurt we inflict on each other. If we seek to understand and identify those differences, we will have a greater desire to accept one another in love.

The first and foremost difference among human beings is identified in Genesis 1:27:

"...<u>male and female</u> created He them."

LEFT BRAIN – RIGHT BRAIN

It is no secret that men and women are uniquely different. We assume that typical men are left brain types who think logically, sequentially and analytically. We assume women are right brain thinkers who are emotionally based. Obviously, this is not always true with every individual, but generally speaking it is the norm. Therefore, there are immediate differences in how a male will tackle a situation versus the way a female does. How a problem is solved or even viewed has much to do with an individual's way of thinking.

Looking at an issue from an emotional point of view will bring entirely different options than when looking at it from a logical point of view. It affects a parent's method of raising children. It affects the manner in which finances are handled. It affects how a discussion or argument will be approached and handled.

I cannot begin to count the number of times my wife, Jeni, has encouraged me to stop at a gas station and ask directions when I am not quite sure of where I am. Females cannot seem to understand the inner motivation that compels a male to get somewhere on his own. Is this pride? Is it simply an inner motivational sense God has placed within us as males? What can possibly cause us to drive miles out of the way, drain the gas tank and get us to our destination a half hour late? Without a doubt, this soon becomes a frustration to the female gender. **IT'S NOT JUST MEN!**

An example of something about the female gender which the typical male does not understand is P.M.S. How can a male comprehend the emotions some females have on a monthly basis? How can he possibly fathom why they are crying without a reason? How can he explain why she does not want a hug even though she is crying? Why is she unable to talk about what she is feeling? Why is it she will not let him fix her problem? Ah, some of the great mysteries of life!

Why do wives get in a "cleaning mode"? Why are some husbands unable to understand the importance of having a clean house? Why does she not seem to appreciate the toaster I got her for Christmas? Why does a man always want tools instead of a really nice sweater? Why does he feel he has to drive 375 miles before stopping on this trip? Why do females need to stop at every interesting outlet mall when he is simply trying to get to his destination? Can anyone understand why a man will not talk about what he is feeling? Why does a woman always need to talk about what she is feeling? The list could go on and on and on.

OPPORTUNITY TO GIVE AND FORGIVE

The obvious differences between the sexes provide us with ample opportunities to forgive each other. We did not choose our gender. Some of the characteristics associated with gender, both physical and emotional, simply come with the package. Because of that fact, males and females react differently to different situations. Whether married or single, gender is a factor in all of our lives.

When others react to a situation differently from the way we react, we can be made to feel that our way is wrong. Others can minimize our opinions and laugh at our reactions or choices. We can feel ignorant, stupid or "not with it".

The opposite is also true. We may be the one to put down someone else's opinions or laugh at them. We may have the

85

opinion we are right and our way of looking at things is the only way. These kinds of attitudes create relationship problems as well.

When God created us, He created males and females to be different from each other. We simply do not think, communicate and react in the same ways. If we can understand that males and females "think" differently and "feel" differently, we can learn to accept these differences.

The next time someone hurts our feelings or makes us defensive, we might ask ourselves if this is a "gender" thing. If it is, then we can begin the practice of granting them mercy and forgiveness for something they certainly did not have under their control. God chose their gender and gave them all the differences associated with it.

Rarely does a marriage consist of a male and female with similar spiritual understanding or convictions. There are times when one of them may be spiritually converted and the other may not have a faith. That will bring a unique set of differences that are not easily reconciled. In these types of situations, all of the things we learned about male and female differences apply, but an additional set of issues enter this unique union.

In 1 Corinthians 7, the Bible tells us the believing husband or wife may be instrumental in the saving of the soul of their spouse. If this does not occur, the believing spouse carries guilt from satan, the accuser. Satan is quick to point out:

- You have not been a good example
- You have not prayed sincerely enough
- God is not honoring His promises
- Not having a believing spouse is unfair
- God is a respecter of persons
- God does not care about your life situation
- (As a wife) You should not submit to your husband since he is not a Believer

This type of scenario quite simply identifies yet another opportunity for a male and female to extend grace and mercy to one another. It is important for us to consider how to handle differences *before* they occur. Reality teaches us that differences most certainly will occur. Are we prepared to handle them when they come? To be forewarned is to be forearmed.

How do you handle conflict situations when someone is an exact opposite of your personality? Do you rebel, get defensive, have hurt feelings, or admire that persons strengths? The following chapter will assist in identifying personality differences as well as giving some hints on how to deal with them.

- 8 -

PERSONALITY DIFFERENCES

HELPFUL REVELATIONS

A young wife shared with me one of her frustrations about her husband. It was a frustration I had heard several times before from a number of other wives. As a wife, she was feeling very inadequate, insecure and taken for granted. She told me her husband never complimented her on anything she did well. He did not compliment her on her appearance, or for that matter, he did not compliment her on virtually any area of her life. She felt she had no worth. She <u>knew</u> she received no compliments because she had no qualities worthy of praise. She was frustrated and was not looking forward to her future years with a husband who did not appreciate her.

We were able to spend some time together identifying her husband's personality profile as well as her own. It is always a glorious time when I see the light of understanding begin to twinkle and then glow in another person. I saw it happen in this young lady.

When she was finally able to see on paper, in black and white just how different their two personalities really were, she began to understand. We should never forget to apply the following verse as it pertains to our differences:

John 8:32: And ye shall know the truth, and the truth shall make you free.

One of the personality characteristics of this particular husband was his tendency to not be complimentary. It was there in black and white for her to see! God did not give him the nature to be complimentary. It was not that she was undeserving of compliments; it was simply not his nature to give them. What a revelation for this wife to know she was not the issue!

For some people, the revelation may be as quick as flipping a light switch. Realistically, more often it is a gradual process taking more time.

COMPOUNDING HURT

She had two personality weaknesses which contributed to some of the struggles in their relationship. One was her "oversensitivity". The other was her "need for compliments".

Understanding the personality differences between them allowed her the privilege of forgiving him for his insensitivities. She began to understand she did have worth and the lack of hearing about it from her husband was not her issue. She began to feel compassion for his lack of sensitivity. She came to realize he missed out on blessings in life because of his inability to feel and express emotions.

As she came to understand him more completely, she learned to appreciate his ability to cut through emotional issues very quickly. This quality made him a great decision maker and leader. He did not get bogged down by the emotions surrounding an issue. He could cut to the chase.

By understanding each of their weaknesses and strengths, she was able to grant him grace and mercy. When we are able to understand each other, we develop compassion for one another.

PERSONALITY CONFLICTS

It seems many conflicts occur due to personality differences. Many different books have been written on the subject of personality profiling. Some are rather basic, while others are very extensive. There are many benefits to understanding basic personalities:

- It can defuse many conflicts.
- It can bring peace to misunderstandings.
- It can bring understanding to our confusion.
- It can bring a peaceful resolution to frustrating problems.
- It can provide healthy self-worth by allowing us to see ourselves as God created us.
- It can bring a willingness to accept others when we see how God made them unique and special.
- It can reveal our individuality.
- It can bring contentment with who God made us to be.

As we learn our own personality weaknesses, we understand how we can be an irritation to others. As we begin to understand other's personality weaknesses, we see how they can irritate us.

When we know other people's personality weaknesses and come to know our own, we understand where arguments, misunderstandings and conflicts come from. Our knowledge of the personality types can bring resolution to the conflicts of life.

ARE PERSONALITIES GOD-GIVEN?

The Scripture gives us a clear understanding of who was in charge of Creation. Quite simply, God tells us He made us the way He wants us to be and thus we need to accept ourselves.

Exodus 4:11: And the Lord said unto him, Who hath made man's mouth? or who maketh the dumb, or deaf, or the seeing, or the blind? have not I the Lord?

Romans 9:20: Nay but, O man, who art thou that repliest against God? Shall the thing formed say to him that formed it, Why hast thou made me thus?

As we consider personality types, we must understand a basic theological truth found in:

Genesis 1:26: And God said, Let us make man in our *image*, after our *likeness*...

In the original Hebrew language, *"image"* specifically related to what would be a "shadow or resemblance." It would be what we see when we look at our reflection in a mirror or on a quiet pond. Image deals with our *physical* characteristics. Sometimes when a baby is born, we hear grandpa say, "She is the image of her mother."

The term *"likeness"* is similar but relates more to "manner" and "the nature of man." We can think of *image* as the physical characteristics of man and *likeness* as his *mental*, *emotional* and *spiritual* side. Therefore, when God provided each of us with a personality and appearance, it was His choosing. He chose to make us look like Him and to have an emotional, mental and spiritual dimension like Him.

There is no such thing as a "wrong" or "bad" personality. God does not make mistakes.

CATEGORIZING

Trying to put an individual's personality into a category is similar to trying to put a Holstein cow into either a black _or_ a white category. (For the agriculturally challenged reader, the Holstein cow is the white one with black spots and patterns). Personalities are complex and do not necessarily fit into categories.

However, there are general categories which enable us to better understand who and what we are. They can also help us predict how we will react to a specific situation and why we react a particular way to a specific individual.

The categories may also help us understand why certain people do the things they do and how they will react in a given set of circumstances. Let me add some perspective to this issue of personality and explain how it affects our everyday life.

As I mentioned earlier, there are many tests available which can help us identify our personality types in various ways. There are personality profiling tests which categorize us based upon our responses to color and shapes. There are other tests which group us by how we stand, how we sit, or how we sleep. Some comprehensive tests are so in-depth they place individuals into 1 of 32 or more personality categories. Other tests identify 4 personality profile categories. In yet another test we can determine if we are introverted or extroverted. There are tests which relate the categories in scientific terms or even animal types. One I ran across identifies what type of dog you would be with your personality characteristics.

For ease of understanding we will describe personality profiling using four words to typify four basic personality types. They are _sanguine_, _choleric_, _melancholy_ and _phlegmatic_. The names are not nearly as important as the characteristics of each type.

Some people have a single dominant type. Others have two dominant types. Most of us are blends of two, three or four of the basic types. As we look at the individual characteristics, we begin to see ourselves falling into one or more categories. We also start to see other individuals fall into categories. God certainly used an infinite imagination as He chose to make us all unique.

Sanguine - The sanguine personality tends to:
- Be extroverted.
- Be fun loving.

- Be a "people person."
- Enjoy crowds.
- Enjoy being the center of attention.
- Be colorful.
- Be an "everyone is a friend" type of person.
- Enjoy being around people.
- Think the more people the merrier.
- Believe "Why should we be sad when there is fun to be had."
- Believe sadness only comes when there is nothing to do, no place to go, and no people to associate with.
- Laugh loud, long and hard.
- Be too outgoing for some people.
- Be labeled as a show-off.

Choleric - The choleric personality tends to:
- Be a born leader.
- Be extroverted.
- Be very capable.
- Handle difficult situations very well.
- Enjoy change and handles conflict well.
- Have many opinions on just about everything imaginable.
- Be a self-starter.
- Have great initiative.
- Be highly motivated.
- Be in charge.
- Speak for others.
- Make decisions for others.
- Radiate self-confidence.
- "Run over the top of others" without even knowing it.
- Be goal oriented.
- Not be emotionally based.
- Not give praise or compliments.

- Not show emotions and, in fact, dislikes a show of emotions in others.
- Consider tears as a show of weakness.
- Hurt other people's feelings.

Melancholy - The melancholy personality tends to:
- Be gifted intellectually.
- Enjoy quiet times alone.
- Be gifted in the fine arts of music, art and poetry.
- Be a deep and profound thinker.
- Be detail conscious.
- Be organized.
- Be careful to the point of perfectionism.
- Be resistant to change.
- Have lots of emotions, but has difficulty identifying those emotions.
- Carry guilt and shame.
- Not feel they measure up in many areas of life.
- Need encouragement and affirmation.
- Be negative.
- Be sober.
- Be serious.
- Be introverted.
- Be more easily depressed than others.

Phlegmatic - The phlegmatic personality tends to:
- Relate well one on one with people.
- Be faithful in the duties laid out for them.
- Swing back and forth between extroverted and introverted tendencies.
- Fit in almost anywhere.
- Not stand out in a crowd.
- Feel emotions deeply.

- Be able to identify emotions both for themselves and for others.
- Be able to put emotions into words.
- Be able to feel other people's hurts and emotions.
- Be resistant to change.
- Be overly sensitive at times.
- Be overly defensive.
- Be indecisive.
- Be hurt easily.
- Need encouragement and affirmation.

When we begin to understand personality types, we can begin to predict how we will respond to various people in various circumstances. We likewise will be able to predict with some accuracy how others will react in a variety of circumstances.

We know the old maxim about opposites attracting. We know this to be true, because many of us were attracted to and married to spouses who are very different from us.

For example, Jeni and I are very different. In fact, we are nearly opposites. This has brought some degree of friction into our 35 years of marriage. There is no doubt we have both been stretched out of our comfort zones. If we both had the same personality types, we would have become dull and stagnant. It is impossible to comprehend what Jeni and I would be like if we did not have each other. I simply cannot imagine life without her balance.

God, the wonderful Provider, knows exactly who and what we need in our lives.

Predictable Consequences

There are very predictable conflicts which occur when we find ourselves associated with others of a different personality type. These predictable conflicts bring about automatic and expected responses. It can easily be seen between a man and a wife in marriage, but obviously happens in every kind of relationship imaginable. You can observe personality conflicts between strangers in the grocery check-out line. They can occur in business relationships as well as friendships. Let us look at a few combinations and the expected outcomes.

Choleric husband and Melancholy wife
- He tends to be extroverted and she introverted.
- He will have strong opinions, and she will resent the fact her opinions arc not heard.
- He will be uncomplimentary, and she will need compliments due to her insecurities.
- He will be very self-confident, and she will greatly lack confidence.
- She will be emotional, and he will not understand her feelings.
- She will have tears, and he will see her tears as a weakness.
- He will thrive on change, and she will resist change.
- She will feel inferior, and he will never understand why.
- She will avoid conflict, and he will create and enjoy it.
- It will appear he wins all of their "arguments," and she is the continual loser.

The Results
- She will tend to feel suppressed and hurt by his strong opinions and lack of positive reinforcement.
- She may feel hurt and discouraged and tend to be depressed.
- She will tend to blame herself for any relationship problems.
- She will begin to believe the choleric personality is the ultimate personality to have.
- Since his choleric personality is so vastly different from hers, she will feel very inferior.
- He will feel very frustrated because he is unable to fix his wife. After all, he can do anything.

A Word Picture

- He will be the lightning, thunder and downpour, while she will feel like the puddle at the side of the road.
- She will feel like the shadow at the base of a mountain.

The Cure

The gap of emotions in this combination is wide and can not be bridged easily. It will take a great amount of effort, tenderness and communication on the husband's part to maintain this relationship with his wife.

His homework:

- He will need to show tenderness and compassion.
- He will need to listen instead of talk.
- He will need to listen to her instead of trying to fix her.
- He will need to give quick praise rather than quickly sharing criticism.
- He will need to whisper instead of shout.
- He will need to communicate what he is feeling.
- He will need to patiently encourage her to share her thoughts and feelings.

Her homework:

- She will need to understand the positive attributes of his choleric nature.
- She will need to develop an appreciation for his leadership and decision-making abilities.
- She will need to develop broader shoulders.
- She will need to develop thicker skin.
- She will need to know her own strengths.
- She will need to develop opportunities to use her strengths.

- She will need to develop a contentment for who God made her to be.

Choleric wife and Melancholy husband
- She will tend to be extroverted.
- He will tend to be introverted.
- She will have strong opinions.
- He will resent his opinions not being heard.
- She will be uncomplimentary.
- He will need compliments because of his insecurities.
- He will be emotional.
- She will have a difficult time expressing her emotions.
- She will not understand his emotions.
- He may cry easily.
- She will see tears as a weakness.
- She may resent his weaknesses.
- She will thrive on change.
- He will resist change.
- She will have no problem with conflict and confrontation.
- She will be perceived as "wearing the pants" and being in charge.
- He will feel inferior.
- She will have a strong self-confidence.

The Results
- He will tend to feel suppressed and hurt by her lack of positive reinforcement.
- He may feel hurt and discouraged and tend to be depressed.
- He will tend to feel he is not the leader in his family, and the roles are reversed.

- Not being the leader can bring shame into his life, which may lead to discouragement and depression.
- Since the choleric personality will be dominant and so vastly different than his, he may feel inferior.

A Word Picture
- She will be the lightning, thunder and downpour, while he will feel like the puddle at the side of the road.
- He will feel like the shadow at the base of a mountain.

The gap of emotions in this combination of personalities can not be bridged easily. The perception of role reversal can create a stigma he will find difficult to accept. To be sustained, this relationship will need sensitivity and communication.

The Cure

His homework:

- He will need to develop broader shoulders.
- He will need to develop thicker skin to handle his wife's sharp words and strong opinions.
- He will need to continually share his emotions and learn communication skills.
- It will be important for him to identify his strengths.
- It will be important for him to find opportunities to use his strengths.
- He will need to learn to appreciate her gifts and talents. They can be a balance for them.

Her homework:

- She must learn to appreciate his tenderness and quietness.

- She should recognize his ability to remain quiet in the midst of chaos as an admirable quality.
- She must learn to listen to his moods rather than his words.
- She must learn her touch will mean much more to him than her opinion or words of correction.
- She must learn he will respond to positive reinforcement.
- She must begin to learn the benefits of encouraging him.
- She must begin to learn the benefits of affirming him.

His strengths will be more evident to others, but not so quickly to himself. His ability to appreciate and recognize her strengths, as well as using his own strengths will reduce his perception of a role reversal in their marriage.

Sanguine husband and Melancholy wife

He is very extroverted and would simply love to be at every social function possible. While there, he would not mind being in the center of everything. She, however, needs to be pushed to attend, and when she finally goes, she would feel some automatic resentment towards him. While there, the tendency to remain on the fringe, in the shadows, or in a corner would always be a temptation for her. No matter what time they leave the social event, it will be an hour later than she wanted to leave. On the way home she might begin the conversation with something like:

"Why do you always have to be the center of attention and leave me standing alone?"

"Leave you alone? You are always hanging back and are so unsociable. What do people think when you are so distant?"

"Me unsociable? Everyone has to wonder why you have to be the center of attention. From my corner I could hear your laughter all night!"

"Life is way too short to spend your time moping in a corner."

"Moping? Why wouldn't I hang back? I have a husband who was laughing so loud and making himself look foolish. I am embarrassed for you!"

...and that is just the warm-up session!

The Results
- She thinks life is far too serious and somber for a Christian to be so fun-loving.
- He thinks her demeanor does not reflect the positive traits of Christ.
- She thinks his carefree attitude does not reflect the nature of Christ.
- She wishes he would be more serious.
- He wishes she were more social.

The Cure
The cure for these personality differences is the same as the others - communication and understanding. Our understanding of one another's attributes will greatly assist a resolution. Our ability to communicate our hurts in an appropriate and non-confronting manner will provide positive results.

Choleric husband and Phlegmatic wife
- He is a very goal-oriented type of person.

- He believes the shortest distance between two points is a straight line.
- Getting from point A to point B is not the goal for her. She believes the goal is to learn as much as you can along the way.
- She believes in taking extra time to get to the goal because enjoying the process is very important to her.
- He believes the speed by which you get there is of utmost importance.
- He believes "the end justifies the means". If you step on someone in the process, they simply should have gotten out of the way.
- He is gifted in making decisions.
- She has a problem with making almost any decision.
- He is not overly concerned with emotions.
- She can tend to be overly concerned about emotions to the point of over-sensitivity.
- He is a rather black and white, opinionated person.
- She sees a lot of gray in almost every situation.
- While working on a project, he is not overly concerned if others do not agree with him. "Let's just get it done."
- She is concerned about whose toes are getting stepped on in the process and making sure they are heard and healed before moving on.
- She is a peacemaker.
- She is busy picking up the pieces he has left behind as he achieves the goal.

The Results
- He is frustrated because she is slowing things down.
- She is frustrated because he is hurting someone in the process of getting the job done.
- He is a "things" oriented person.
- She is a "people" oriented person.

- They will greatly differ when making decisions.
- Because of their extreme differences, they will have difficulty in finding common ground.

The Cure
- It will be important for him to understand his emotions.
- It will be important for him to express his emotions.
- It will be important for him to give her time to express her emotions.
- It will be important for him to slow down and be patient.
- She must learn how to think about goals and the end results.

This marriage will have automatic friction and abrasion. There is much this couple can accomplish if they can learn to pull together. The frustrations will cause this couple to resist one another and to withhold things from each other. When they learn teamwork, they will be amazed at how beautiful married life can be.

Choleric husband and Choleric wife
When these two individuals get together, there is no need for a 4th of July celebration! There will be lots of fireworks in this marriage. Both are opinionated, and both can enjoy conflict. Each will think they are "right" and will not give up an argument very easily. For this type of union, try picturing gasoline and a match. With this marriage you may wonder what God had in mind when He brought these two together.

The Results
There can be a lot of friction and conflict in this type of marriage. However, both partners have rather thick skin and broad shoulders. Therefore, the damage is not nearly so severe, nor is

the resentment as long lasting as you might expect. This couple can cause bystanders to think divorce is imminent, while the couple thinks their conflict and subsequent resolution is perfectly normal.

The Cure

As is the case for any personality conflict, communication and understanding are the cure. Understanding one another's attributes will greatly assist resolution of conflicts. It will be beneficial in this case for each partner to permit the other to practice their unique gifts. While they both have the same personality, there will be distinctive spiritual gifts, talents and experiences which will provide uniqueness.

Melancholy husband and Melancholy wife

Since both tend to be introverted, you will not find this couple socially active. They sometimes will go along with the crowd, but they will not be initiators. They will hang back and wait to be invited. Because of their timidity, they may tend to be easily forgotten. Being forgotten will add to their already low self-worth and confidence. They will both be gifted in many ways, but with their introverted personalities, they may never get the opportunity to utilize their gifts.

They are an opportunity waiting to happen. In Christian circles, they need to be encouraged and included. Once secure in their social circle, they will be tremendous assets. However, someone will need to assist them in making this happen.

Within their marriage, they will get along reasonably well together. A common problem for them is that both will tend towards discouragement and depression. Thus, when both hit the low end of emotions at the same time, it is compounded greatly. Unfortunately, their timidity and shyness will keep them away from encouragers and groups where this couple could create great balance.

Choleric Fast Food Restaurant Cashier and Phlegmatic Customer

Can you picture the scene? It is high noon at a fast food restaurant. The crowds are pressing into the small area in front of the four cashiers and their cash registers. The lines are formed with eight hurried and harried customers in each line. The *choleric* cashier is processing the orders quickly, efficiently and methodically. The *phlegmatic* customer has been in line for seven minutes and is now facing her natural personality opposite, the *choleric* cashier. She steps up to the cashier and says...

"Hi, how are you today? Pretty day, isn't it?"

Cashier: "Yes ma'am. Can I take your order *please*?"
Customer: "Oh, yes. What types of chicken sandwiches do you have? I've been shopping *all* morning, and I am as hungry as a bear."
Cashier: (He tells her the five sandwiches in three seconds flat!).
Customer: "That's a big list. What was the third one you mentioned? I'm not sure I know which one is best. You know, with all of the things you put on them, there are *so* many options! Need to be thinking about nutrition and all. Can I order a sandwich plain?"

Cashier: (He is rolling his eyes not so discreetly by now...)

And so the conversation goes...

Melancholy Supervisor and Choleric Employee

The dynamics in this relationship are volatile. The aggressive personality of the employee is threatening to the supervisor. The supervisor may try to restrict the progressive nature of the employee, and in fact, may derail a promotion. The natural insecurity and fears of the supervisor would cause him to have a concern for his own job security.

The obvious results could be an employee who would become very frustrated at the caution and carefulness of his boss. The chances are fairly good the employee would seek employment elsewhere out of frustration.

However, if the employee was aware of personality differences, he would understand the fears and insecurities the melancholy supervisor may be having. In that case, the employee could do things to make his boss look good. Handled carefully, the employee could be well rewarded for his sensitivity and diligence.

SUMMARY

There are obviously many other combinations of personalities we could envision. I will assume at this point you get the picture. Again, our purpose in this exercise is to identify those personality characteristics which make us different from one another. We are always the winner when our understanding of personalities allows us to improve our relationships with others. It becomes intriguing to find ways in which we can forgive those who hurt us.

When we understand the concept that it was God who placed our personalities within us, we realize we need to accept our personality for what it is. Likewise, we understand we have an obligation to allow others to have and to live their God-given personalities.

It is sometimes easy for a sensitive person to become hurt, angry, resentful and even bitter against those who are abrasive to them. After reading this, possibly you can understand how their God given personality may make them insensitive. We can begin to tolerate their natural insensitivity a bit more by learning how their insensitivity can be used for good. We are always in need of people who are able to rise above disaster and trauma. Some of us crumble during those times. Rather than dwelling on their forwardness, we can learn to appreciate their God-given ability to accomplish difficult tasks. God fills the human population with a balance.

Likewise, it may be easy for us to be bothered by those who are indecisive and a bit wishy-washy. However, we do appreciate their God-given talents for detail and taking cautious care of things which we might find cumbersome and menial. We are thankful for those who can put themselves into the shoes of the hurting and help them in their distress. Rather than concentrating on their indecisiveness, let us concentrate on their sensitive hearts. God fills the Earth with a balance.

The next time someone hurts our feelings or makes us defensive, we might ask ourselves if this is a "personality" thing. If it is, then we can begin the practical application of granting them mercy and forgiveness for something not under their control. God chose and created their personality and all the differences associated with it.

We have heard the saying "Walk a mile in my shoes". That cliché causes us to realize we all have different backgrounds and experiences which have formed us to some degree. Just how different is your life from mine? The next chapter explores some of those differences and how to handle them.

- 9 -

BACKGROUNDS AND EXPERIENCES

ROOT ISSUES

In 1986, I had a young mother make an appointment with me. When she arrived, I asked her why she wanted to visit. She said she had a difficult time dealing with anger in her life. She was angry at her children. She was angry with her husband. She was angry with life in general. We looked at the Scriptures that relate to anger. We shared some thoughts. We had a prayer together, and she went on her way.

A year later, she again called to make an appointment. When she arrived, I asked her what she wanted to talk about. She said she had a difficult time dealing with anger in her life. She was angry at her children. She was angry with her husband. She was angry with her life in general. That sparked my memory.

I said, "I thought we dealt with that a year ago?" She said, "Yes, but it didn't help much."

I was frustrated. Having always believed the Bible and prayer would get us through anything and everything, what could I be missing? Fortunately, the Holy Spirit led us back to a root issue. Not having an opportunity to know this young lady until she was 20, I did not know her background. In this second session, I found out she was only in her early teens when her mother passed away. She had to be strong for her father, and thus she did not grieve the loss of her mother. She had developed anger towards her mother for having left her when she needed her the most.

She was angry that her mom was not alive to see her grandchildren. She was angry at God for taking her mother. Over a two month period of counseling together, she grieved deeply.

Eighteen years have passed and we have not needed to talk about anger since. In the process, she has learned how to "forgive" God and accept things that happen in her life. Her husband learned how to show compassion to her, and their marriage is wonderfully balanced and blessed.

I'VE NOT BEEN THERE...!

This chapter is devoted to learning how to cope with others who have different backgrounds and experiences than you may have had. It will teach you how to develop compassion for others and how to be tolerant of them when they hurt you. You can learn to understand why someone's past can dictate their present behavior, as well as predict how they might react to future situations.

How many times do we quickly draw conclusions or make judgments about someone else? Only later do we learn about their background, or learn of a significant experience in their life that shaped them.

In the past I had perceptions and conclusions about what it might be like for someone to lose their father. I would go through a funeral visitation line and give my condolences to young men who had lost their dads. However, when I went through that loss with my own dad in 1997, I realized my prior conclusions, perceptions and condolences were distorted. Once I had made the experience, I was able to understand and then was able to handle future situations in an appropriate way. I learned how to *listen* to those who were grieving rather than talking.

Likewise, I had perceptions of what it was like for a parent to have a child injured. As a pastor, I have had many opportunities to sit with devastated parents at the bedside of their injured or dying child. Until our son experienced traumatic brain injury, I did not have a true understanding of what parents were going through.

Prior to our own experience, I would try to offer advice to hurting parents on how to deal with the issues at hand. I would do the best I could, but reality changed the perceptions Jeni and I had. I came to realize how inaccurate and insensitive my advice must have been to those parents.

I can think of hundreds of experiences in life where I have not had personal experience. Do I have the right to draw hard and fast conclusions about things I have not experienced? Dare I tell parents who have just lost a child in a car accident, "She is in a better place" or "Just let this increase your faith"? How would those statements make the parents feel? Unfortunately, there are times we draw wrong conclusions or make erroneous judgments because of a lack of our own experiences.

DIG DEEPER...

When I was twelve years old, I worked for my uncle during the summer months. My job was to hoe the weeds and thistles out of his acres and acres of soybeans and corn. He took me to a remote field, let me out of his car and gave me the instructions for the day. "Make sure when you hoe the Canadian Thistles you get the roots. Otherwise they will grow right back."

It was a hot, hot day. Going swimming seemed like a really fun thing to do. I hurried through the field, not paying much attention to thistle roots. It soon became easier to cut those ugly brutes off at ground level than it was to get the roots. After all, from the road, who would know whether the roots were gone or not? My work was accomplished so I went swimming.

A week later, my uncle picked me up to hoe another field. On the way, he took me to that earlier field and pointed to a thriving batch of Canadian Thistles. I received another lesson that day about "roots"! Those thistles had grown back in all their glory! My lack of dedication and motivation had found me out.

113

GET THE ROOTS!

The experience I mentioned at the beginning of this chapter about the young mother with an anger issue changed the way I looked at life. That day, I learned not to draw hasty conclusions from what I see or hear. I have learned when someone comes for counseling; the issue they tell me about is rarely the issue we need to discuss. Generally, the problem they share is only a symptom of an unresolved and much deeper hurt. I have learned to ask myself: Is anger really the root issue? Is an eating disorder the root issue? Is envy the root issue? Is a relationship problem with their father the root issue? Is an addiction to tobacco, drugs, alcohol or sex really the root issue?

If we can understand root issues are not apparent, then we can learn to refrain from judging one another. If, when someone hurts us, we can conclude there are things in their background and past we simply do not know about, then we can give them the benefit of the doubt. We can grant them mercy and compassion much quicker. We learn how to cope with others who have had different experiences in their lives than we have had. As our sympathy grows, misunderstandings disappear. When our empathy increases, hurts diminish. When compassion develops, bitterness, resentment and anger leave.

EXPERIENCES MOLD US

There are so many things that make us who and what we are. Most of those things are God-given and beyond our control. Our gender, parents, siblings, personality, gifts, and appearance are all things we did not ask for and thus are not under our control.

Backgrounds and experiences are only partly within our control. We can make some decisions which create new experiences for us and thus become new background for our lives. We cannot say that background is only God's issue. We do have some control of and responsibility for our actions. However, we can say our background, regardless of the origin, does have an

114

impact on the present as well as our future. We need to remember that today's actions become tomorrow's experiences.

After you had read Chapter 1 about my background and experiences regarding the first 18 years of my life, you could understand how those experiences shaped me. As of January 1, 2004, it was estimated the world population was 6, 339, 384, 914. Therefore, besides mine, there are another 6, 339, 384, 913 illustrations which are uniquely different from anyone else on the face of the Earth.

You could understand why my experiences had a profound impact on who and what I am. If you would have met me after reading Chapter 1, and I pushed your button in a conversation, you would now be fairly quick to forgive me or give me the benefit of the doubt. You could do that by thinking - "He still has some insecurities because of those years of rejection"; "He must still have some things to work through"; or "I am glad I did not have to go through what Ed went through." I thank you in advance for understanding how to cope with my rough edges. We are learning together the concept of our human differences and the granting of mercy to those who are different from us.

Some might say developing tolerance or acceptance of others who are different from us "enables" them to continue on in their negative emotions, attitudes or lifestyles. There is always a need for proper confrontation as we read in Matthew chapter 18. However, when our feelings are hurt and wounded, and we are angry or defensive, we are not Biblically or emotionally prepared to confront, challenge or even caution those who may have wounded us.

As Believers, we are to remove or at least minimize our hurt feelings and defensiveness so we can be what God wants us to be. We can be effective tools for Him, when we get our own emotions and wounded spirit out of the way.

Let us look at some illustrations so we can better understand this concept of understanding differences and subsequently granting mercy.

PHYSICAL ABUSE

First of all, let us look at a little boy who was raised in a home where physical abuse was extensive. The boy's father was abusive to his wife, as well as to his children. Have we been through this kind of trauma? If not, then we need to understand how this child would have issues to deal with as an adult.

Would this now adult male have struggles with relationships? Would he have a warped understanding of what a father and son relationship might be like? Would he understand the concept of unconditional love? Would he have a healthy respect for his wife? Would there potentially be some unresolved anger issues in his life? Would he be prone to physically abusing others? After being converted, will he be able to feel a healthy love and acceptance from God, his heavenly Father? Will he be thinking of God as a terrifying creature who is quick to judge and punish?

How can we possibly judge the actions, reactions, inactions or statements of someone who grew up in a home such as this if we did not? Is it possible your path crossed someone like that today?

Are any of these hurting people at our work, the person who cut us off in traffic, or the person who butted into line ahead of us at the fast food restaurant? Did our path cross their path today? If so, what was our reaction? Did we think there was no excuse for their behavior? Or possibly, did we wonder what happened to them as children to make them act this way as adults? Could you have rubbed shoulders with someone like that today?

ABSENT FATHER

Let us consider another illustration. Imagine a little girl who was raised in a home where the father was absent because of a divorce or possibly because he worked countless hours. In any case, he was not around for the daily family life. How will this child react as an adult?

116

Were we raised in a home such as this? If not, then we need to understand how this little girl would have issues to deal with when she became an adult. Will this woman be searching the rest of her life, for a father's love? Will she be searching for closeness and intimacy? If she marries, will she be able to accept her husband's love and intimacy? Will she enjoy that closeness, but always fear he may leave?

Are we hasty to be critical of the actions, reactions, inactions or statements of someone who grew up in a home such as this? Could you have rubbed shoulders with someone like that today?

NO POSITIVE AFFIRMATION

Think about children who are raised in a home where they never received positive reinforcement or encouragement. Can we relate? If not, then we need to understand how these children would have issues to deal with as adults. Will they feel secure or will they have feelings of insecurity? Will that insecurity cause them to be defensive and struggle with hurt feelings? Will there be issues of low self-worth they struggle with for the balance of their life? Will they feel anger towards their parents when they find other children who have a healthy self-worth? Will they have difficulty accepting compliments or encouragement from others? Will they feel bitterness for not having loving and affirming parents? Will that bitterness twist into anger towards others?

Are we hasty to be critical of the actions, reactions, inactions or statements of someone who grew up in a home such as this? Could you have rubbed shoulders with someone like that today?

LEGALISTIC RELIGION

How about those who grew up in a home where religion was taught in a legalistic manner? A home where God was viewed with fear without the balance of love? An environment where judgment was just a quick step behind a failure or mistake? A home where the abundant life of Jesus Christ was not conveyed? A home where a child was taught salvation was earned by doing good works? Can we relate? If not, then we need to understand how these children can have issues to deal with when they become adults.

What will the future be like for a child raised in this type of atmosphere? Will they consider God's love as unconditional? Will they see Him through eyes of fear? Will they feel so insecure about their salvation they will not be able to experience the joy, peace and abundance of the Christian walk? Will they be so filled with a fear of failure they will be unable to have an outreach or ministry of their own? Will they ever experience the joy of a sanctified and abundant life? Will they have perfectionist attitudes? Will anyone ever be able to do something good enough to please them? Will they be quick to judge others? Will they be swift to place blame?

Are we quick to judge the actions, reactions, inactions or statements of someone who grew up in a home such as this? Could you have rubbed shoulders with someone like that today?

SEXUAL ABUSE

Sexual abuse causes some of the deepest and most profound wounds a child can experience. Children who have been sexually abused will deal with issues of trust and shame to some degree for the rest of their lives. Let us consider children who were sexually abused at the age of six, nine or thirteen. Did this unspeakable and horrific set of experiences happen to any of us? If not, then we need to understand how children will have issues to deal with when they become adults.

Will they ever learn to fully trust? Will they ever be able to experience intimacy? Will their sexual life be healthy? Will they learn the concept of unconditional love? Will they permit

118

their children to be out from under their control? Will they ever trust anyone to care for their children? Will their wounded spirits cause them to lash out at others in anger?

Are we quick to judge the actions, reactions, inactions or statements of someone who grew up in a home such as this? Could you have rubbed shoulders with someone like that today?

ON AND ON AND ON...

The list of illustrations could go on and on and on. We each have had our own specific sets of experiences. Since we desire others to grant us mercy and compassion for our own past we have the responsibility of offering that mercy to others. It is healthy for us to understand how different we really are from each other. When we understand this, we are able to grant mercy to and have tolerance for others. We likewise will be better able to give others the benefit of the doubt.

Are these illustrations extreme? Unfortunately, they are not. They are real and are happening on a daily basis. Some hurts are greater and some are lesser. However, each set of hurtful experiences cause emotional wounds, injured hearts and damaged lives. Each individual will have a tendency to react differently to each future situation, because of that hurt. When those wounded individuals make us angry or hurt us with statements or actions, we can learn to develop compassion for them. We forgive them as we gain in our understanding of others. The realities of this world give us ample opportunity for giving others the benefit of the doubt.

Unfortunately, we do not know the backgrounds and experiences of many people who lash out at us, step on our toes, stab us in the back or hurt us. When we do know there is a wounded heart behind the tongue lashing we just received, it is easier to grant mercy towards them. However, we do not always know our antagonist's background. If we can assume everyone who hurts us is carrying some type of concealed wound, granting mercy can become an attitude and a lifestyle for us.

119

The ability to grant mercy brings healing and peace.

When we spend time with someone who seems greatly gifted, we may tend to admire them or we may resent them. The area in which we are gifted tends to impact our reaction to those gifted differently than ourselves. What are those gifts and how should we react to those who are different than us? The next chapter will provide some insight.

122

- 10 -

SPIRITUAL GIFTS

When I was young, it was very easy for me to cry. I was often called a cry-baby. Tears were never too far under the surface. I hated that part of myself. Because I still had a tendency to cry easily when I hit the teenage years, I tried to build some walls around my heart to keep that sensitivity away. Satan was readily available with his devices to provide ways for me to harden my heart.

I am so thankful God's Holy Spirit can crumble walls and soften hearts in spite of our efforts to keep Him out.

During those years of hating that sensitive part of myself, I counted my sensitivity as a liability. Only much later did I learn that the sensitivity within me was a spiritual gift called "mercy."

Today, I know I have that gift within me. I likewise know God placed it within me and I had nothing to do with creating, nurturing or using it. There are six simple questions we can ask ourselves in recognizing a spiritual gift.

- Does it seem natural?
- Is it pleasant?
- Is it useful?
- Is it something I need to constantly nurture?
- Is it something I needed to search for and seek after?
- Does using it bring a sense of fulfillment to me?

GOD'S BUSINESS

It is not unusual for devout born-again Christians to be uncertain of their spiritual gifts. It is also not abnormal for many to desire a gift that is different from the one God has given them. The spiritual gifts outlined in the Scriptures are wonderful tools God uses to reach others and meet needs here on Earth. They are very different. How could they be otherwise? In a diverse world of unique people, it takes various gifts to reach the hearts of everyone.

We will take some time to examine the spiritual gifts outlined in the Scripture. We need to explore this topic, because these gifts are very different and in many cases opposite from each other. Gifts can become an area of "difference" in a marriage, friendship or a business environment, thus creating conflict.

Our understanding of the diversity of spiritual gifts can defuse some of the differences among us. These diversities and differences can be used to enhance relationships and neutralize conflict. Understanding gifts gives us coping skills, as we learn to tolerate others whose gifts are different from ours.

Paul gives us instruction regarding spiritual gifts in:

1 Corinthians 12:1: Now concerning spiritual gifts, brethren, I would not have you ignorant.

It is God's desire for us as born-again Believers, to know (and not be ignorant) about the gifts He has placed within us.

How many times have people told you they really appreciate your willingness to serve others? Possibly they state how much they appreciate your ability to teach? How many times do you minimize those compliments with statements like, "Oh, it's nothing. It was such a little thing."

Is it difficult for us to receive compliments? If it is, it reveals a spiritual truth.

Let us ponder a question. Is it pride to accept a compliment? Is it pride to turn a compliment away? As Bible-believing Christians, we never want to be guilty of arrogance or pride. Possibly we turn away compliments about our gifts because we do not want anyone to think we are arrogant or proud. But, when we look at the next three verses of Scripture, we will understand those gifts within us are God's doing, not our own:

Romans 12:6: Having then gifts differing according to *the grace that is given to us...*

1 Corinthians 12:11: But all these (gifts) worketh that one and the selfsame Spirit, (God) dividing to every man severally *as He will*.

1 Corinthians 12:18: But now hath *God* set the members every one of them in the body, *as it hath pleased him*.

No man yet has taken credit for Niagara Falls, the Grand Canyon, DNA, the Milky Way Galaxy or the Swiss Alps. We know to whom the glory goes and why. Likewise, it is appropriate to respond to those who recognize the presence of the God-given gifts within us. Minimizing those compliments is a discredit to the Creator.

When we realize the gifts within us are designed, given and nurtured by Him, we can understand it is appropriate to acknowledge them. It is appropriate because He gets the glory for what He has chosen to do with His creation.

WHO AND WHAT AM I?

There are two basic questions to ask in our search to know who and what we are:

1. What are my gifts?

2. Where did I get my gifts?

When those two questions are answered through His Holy Spirit, we can be at peace with who and what we are. There will be countless opportunities to use those gifts, and we will be spiritually fulfilled. When we learn about our gifts, we will be more able to readily accept the gifts of others and simply accept others as being "different."

It is just as important for us to recognize the gifts we have, as it is to recognize those gifts we do not possess.

Let us take a look at the seven gifts outlined in Romans Chapter 12.

Romans 12:6-8: Having then gifts differing according to the grace that is given to us, whether **prophecy**, let us prophesy according to the proportion of faith; [7] Or **ministry**, let us wait on our ministering: or he that teacheth, on **teaching**; [8] Or he that exhorteth, on **exhortation**: he that **giveth**, let him do it with simplicity; he that **ruleth**, with diligence; he that sheweth **mercy**, with cheerfulness.

As we explore each of the seven gifts outlined in Scripture, we will be able to more readily identify those which are within us. There is no question God places spiritual gifts within each of His children for His purpose and business. Our gifts are treasures waiting to be discovered. They are riches waiting to be shared.

Prophecy

Our initial idea of the spiritual gift of prophecy might slant towards the concept of predicting or prophesying the future. The original Greek language bears that out. However, as we explore the lives of the powerful prophets of old, we read of their experiences in the Old Testament. Through the direction of God, they delivered many "if/then" statements to Israel, Judah and individuals. For instance, we read:

Jeremiah 12:17: But _if_ they will not obey, _(then)_ I will utterly pluck up and destroy that nation, saith the Lord.

The Old Testament books are full of prophetic statements. Today, this gift of prophecy is represented by several characteristics:

- Prophets tend to be great discerners.
- Prophets or discerners are apt to be black and white in their opinions.
- Prophets are likely to be strongly opinionated.
- Prophets tend to be confident.
- They can easily see cause and effect.
- They can foresee consequences to specific actions.
- They will probably be the people who will challenge leadership on issues.
- It is not easy for them to allow "wrong" to continue.
- They are apt to concentrate on the sin rather than the sinner.
- They may at times seem to be insensitive, unloving, tactless and uncaring.
- They are likely to be the individuals who warn people of danger.

Once a prophet or discerner senses danger or wrong, they must sound the warning, otherwise they will have difficulty living with themselves.

Ministry

This gift deals with the natural ability to "serve." The original Greek would translate - "attending as a servant." We all know individuals who continually serve others. Their goal and gift in life is to take care of the needs of others. Luke Chapter 10 describes Martha. Martha was one of the classic servers in the Bible.

People with the gift of ministry or serving are characterized by several distinctive traits:

- "Service with a smile".
- Their joy and fulfillment in life comes from meeting the needs of others.
- They live to serve.
- They love to make life easier for others.
- Many times they simply do not know when or how to say "no."
- They will serve others at the expense of their own energy and health.

We have all seen the cartoons of a dog bringing the slippers and newspaper to his master. After delivering the items, the dog, content with a pat on the head, sits at the feet of his master. It is not much different for people with the gift of ministry. They receive great joy by making life easier for others.

Teaching

Individuals who have the gift of teaching are characterized by several unique traits:

- They have an instinctive desire to read and learn.
- Teachers have a natural ability to deliver knowledge and information in a manner easily understood by others.
- Their desire to obtain knowledge is generally as strong as the desire to impart it to someone else.
- They enjoy being in an environment of learning.

- They take pleasure rather than pride in sharing their knowledge with others.
- The teacher's goal is not to appear knowledgeable, but rather that they can impart information to assist others.
- Teachers are usually great communicators.
- They are effective in classroom settings or any environment where people want to learn.
- A truly gifted teacher feels strongly he must teach truth.

Exhortation

The original Greek would define exhortation as "calling someone near so they can be encouraged." When we feel encouraged by someone, we know we have been in the presence of an exhorter.

The typical traits we can see in those who are gifted with natural exhortation are:

- The ability to comfort, console and give solace with words to those who are hurting.
- The ability to comfort, console and give solace by merely being present.
- Once a need has been identified, the exhorter knows how to minister to that person.
- The exhorter utilizes a variety of ways to encourage. They may use stories, illustrations and parables to share their encouragement.

Giving

There are a variety of qualities we can readily see in those naturally gifted with giving:

- They quickly see needs in others.
- They are quick to meet those needs.
- Their giving is unselfish and generous.

- They give of their time, resources and money.
- They do not desire recognition for their good works.
- They find fulfillment in their giving and sharing.
- It is important for a giver to know their resources will be utilized wisely.

Ruling

The original Greek would describe ruling as, "standing before; presiding; to be over; to rule."

We can easily recognize the gift of ruling in people via several unique characteristics:

- They have an ability to manage and direct people.
- Their talent in administration, organization and implementation is easily recognized.
- They recognize a need and can quickly organize a committee to accomplish the project.
- Leadership comes naturally.
- Others appreciate their management and ability to give direction.

Mercy

The original Greek word implies "mercy, compassion and pity.'

The mercy gifted person is easily recognized by several distinctive characteristics:

- The individual gifted with mercy has an ability to recognize someone who is hurting.
- They have an ability to feel the pain of others.
- They will sense what it is like to walk in someone else's shoes.
- They are able to sense the deep emotional needs of someone who is hurting.
- They know how to help and assist.

- They can feel compassion and pity very easily for the hurting person.
- In a crowd, they will gravitate to the hurting, lonely and wounded hearts.
- They will be able to determine whether touch, words or tears will give the most comfort to injured individuals.

GIFT COMPATIBILITIES

There are several gifts which seem to go hand in hand. It is not uncommon to find the following combinations in the same person.

- The gifts of prophecy and ruling.
- The gifts of exhorting and mercy.
- The gifts of ministry (serving) and giving.

LACK OF GIFT COMPATIBILITIES

However, to the contrary, there are gifts that repel like oil and water. Prophecy and mercy are extreme opposites. Generally you will not find an individual gifted with both prophecy and mercy. A relationship between someone gifted with mercy and someone gifted with prophecy usually creates conflict.

Similarly, someone who has a strong gift of giving, usually will conflict with someone who does not have that gift. Their giving can create issues. The giver wishes to give with a freedom of heart, while the other may be a server and may want to give time. This environment creates conflict and provides an opportunity for each to practice patience and forbearance.

OPPORTUNITIES TO PRACTICE MERCY

Our understanding of one another's spiritual gifts allows us the privilege to grant grace and mercy and to forgive others when they hurt us.

Be assured, in almost every case when others have pushed our button, we are probably doing the same to them. When a spiritually gifted "prophet" irritates a "mercy-gifted" person, we can believe the "mercy" gift is likewise irritating to the prophet. When a mercy-gifted person feels irritated by a prophets harsh dealing with sin, it is likely the prophet is feeling irritated by the mercy-gifted person and his perceived softness with sin.

GIFTS FROM GOD

Recognizing that spiritual gifts are given to each of us by our Creator, is the beginning of understanding. If we realize God gave someone a particular gift, we recognize we must allow God to use that gift in them. Since God gives us a particular gift, we understand it is our reasonable duty to let Him use it in us. Spiritual gifts are tremendous tools He desires to use to build His kingdom. What are your gifts?

Example

I recently met with a young woman who is married and has three children. She was struggling with her view of herself. She felt unworthy of God's love, as well as believing she lacked gifts and talents. It went without saying that she was also struggling with her perception of who God is and how God sees her.

Issues of our self-worth and our image of God seem to go hand in hand.

I asked this mother to take time during the next week to make a list of her unique gifts and talents. I instructed her to write of the positive things she was seeing in herself. When she did that, she was utterly amazed!

When I asked what the experience was like, she said, "I didn't know I had so many gifts!" Then as an afterthought, she said, "That sounds really arrogant, doesn't it?"

When we are able to view our gifts and talents as *God-given*, we have no false sense of pride or arrogance. Conversely, it is fair to say when we do not recognize those gifts and talents as being God given, we have a false humility. A fear of pride can cause us to have this false humility and thus diminish our usefulness.

MISSING GIFTS

We will now explore how to deal with the gifts we do not have. It is just as important to know the gifts we do not have as it is to know our gifts. The lack of a particular gift is not important.

When we try to excel in a gift we do not have, we become discouraged and frustrated. Trying to be something we are not promotes feelings of unworthiness, failure and fatigue.

People, who are part of a church congregation filled with excellent servers, will wear out trying to keep up with those God-gifted servers. If we have great admiration for someone with a certain gift, we tend to be too hard on ourselves if we do not have the same gift. There are many Christian Believers who want to be someone other than who God made them to be. I was a classic example.

My personality is phlegmatic. My spiritual gifts are exhorting and mercy. I have always had a tender and sensitive heart. I was called "cry-baby" more than once in my life. My tears are usually just below the surface. There was a period of time when I admired strong people with unemotional demeanors and personalities. For a period of about two years, I tried to mimic those traits. Those were two of the most miserable years of my life!

ACCEPTING OUR GIFTS

When we are able to see benefit from our gifts, we can generally accept them. This can happen when someone tells you their lives have been changed by our service, giving, mercy,

133

compassion, challenging, or teaching. When we can see the effectiveness of one of our gifts, we can have spiritual fulfillment.

We generally know our gifts by the manner in which things flow naturally and those areas in which they do not. For instance, I am not gifted in the teaching area. Teaching is work for me. Nor am I a ministry-gifted person, because doing "things" for others does not come naturally for me. Prophecy is not one of my gifts, as I am not black and white or a confrontation natured person. In fact, I see many shades of gray in most areas and look for other roads to peace rather than confrontation.

However, there is an area that comes very naturally to me, and that area brings me the greatest amount of satisfaction. Because of His gift, it is natural for me to feel the pain of others. A hurting or struggling person in a crowd stands out when there is nothing on their face to indicate hurt. It is a natural reaction for me to identify root emotional issues in someone's life after listening to them for a few minutes. Beyond all of that, I enjoy it and it becomes my passion. Sharing that gift provides fulfillment and energizes me, rather than draining me of energy.

Again, it is just as important for me to know my God-given gifts as it is to know those I do not have. I would waste considerable amounts of time and joy by trying to be good at things I am not gifted in. I believe God wants us to spend our time in those areas in which He has gifted us.

It is essential for us to be all God has created us to be – no more, no less!

This chapter has been devoted as much to learning about ourselves as it has been devoted to learning about others. As a mercy-gifted person, I am very opposite from a prophecy-gifted person. Prophets can be a frustration to me because they can sometimes hurt a vulnerable person without even being aware.

I have learned, however, that a prophet's gift is just as God given, effective and as important as the one God gave me and others. Knowing this, allows me the privilege of accepting them for who they are.

Can you imagine how frustrating I am to the prophet-gifted person? As they see me grant mercy and compassion to someone, they must think I am enabling that person to continue in their struggles and problems. While the prophet is saying, "This is the problem, and here is how to get over it," I am saying "Let's back off and give this person some room. Can't you see they are hurting, and need some tender care, compassion and love?"

How frustratingly slow and shallow I must seem to prophet-gifted people! I trust they are developing tolerance for me as I learn to do that for them. Just understanding their gift is God given helps me to pause, step back and listen to them. They are so gifted in discerning and cutting to the chase. This provides such a balance.

THE EXTREMES

While we have talked about the application of spiritual gifts, we dare not forget there are misapplications as well. A mercy-gifted person can show so much mercy that sin can be overlooked. A ministry or serving-gifted person can do so much for others that others are encouraged to become lazy. A teaching-gifted person can soon look down on others who do not desire knowledge as much as they do.

The application of this is rather straightforward:

- Understand all gifts are God-given.
- Identify the gifts God has given you.
- Identify the gifts which God has not given you.
- Develop tolerance for those with different gifts by letting them be who God wants them to be.

135

- Be prayerful you will not seek the gifts God chose not to give you.
- Be prayerful you will not be jealous of those who have a gift you do not have.
- Be prayerful He will give you opportunities to use the gifts you do have.
- Be prayerful you will not misapply and misuse the gifts God has given you.

Another aspect of our life has to do with our personal likes and dislikes. There are things which fulfill and enrich us and things which do not. That creates yet another area making us unique and different from one another. How do you handle those who have very different "likes" and "dislikes"? Chapter 11 will investigate the process of enrichment and fulfillment.

- 11 -

FULFILLMENT

THE RAPTURE FACTOR

During the time Jeni and I were engaged in 1969, she celebrated her 20th birthday. I asked my mom what I should get Jeni for her birthday. Mom thought a dozen roses would be really nice. That seemed wise to me because I could remember the glow on my mother's face when Dad would bring her cut flowers. That glow remained on my mother's face for days, or so it seemed to me!

As I was growing up, I can remember the expression of great pleasure, delight and rapture on my mother's face when she received something which made her very happy. I call those times the Rapture Factor.

ANXIOUS ANTICIPATION

So, with great eagerness, I followed my mother's advice and took a dozen roses to Jeni. Ah, the aroma and beauty of those roses as their scent filled my car on the 15-mile trip to her house! I was anxiously looking forward to the great pleasure, delight and rapture on her face indicating the Rapture Factor. I walked into her home and made the grand presentation. Jeni loved the roses and was thankful I had remembered her birthday.

BUT...

But in spite of her thankfulness for my having remembered her birthday, there was no Rapture Factor. In spite of her love for the fragrance of the roses, there was no Rapture Factor. In spite of her appreciation of the natural beauty of the flowers, there was no Rapture Factor.

Why? Could something possibly be wrong with the flowers? How could the wisdom of my mother fail me at a time like this?

THE DELIGHT BLIGHT

The dictionary describes blight as: "A condition which impedes growth and promotes wilting." What I saw on Jeni's face that day was a wilting of her happy expectations. I knew then that something else was going on when she reacted differently than my mother would have. I was seeing the dreaded Delight Blight!

DIFFERENCES ARE GOOD?

When Jeni and I talked about it, I was able to understand why she was a little disappointed. First of all, she was very thankful I remembered her birthday and brought flowers. However, since finances were a bit tight for us and cut flowers wither and die within a week, something else more lasting might have been more economical and practical.

I learned something that day about the unspoken laws of the Rapture Factor or the Delight Blight. That day, September 10, 1969, I learned different things make different people glow. Receiving cut flowers was not one of those things which would make Jeni glow.

That occurrence so many years ago taught me much about the differences God gave each of us to define us and make us unique. He knew if I could easily please Jeni by something as simple as periodically bringing her cut flowers, I would probably get careless and sloppy. So, He provided me with a wife who would stretch me.

140

I had to ask myself, "What can I do for Jeni that will make her happy?" What an imagination God must have! I had no idea where that question would take me! It took me into the dreaded...

NO MAN'S LAND

I have learned over the course of time that cleaning the garage is a sure way to produce the Rapture Factor for Jeni. Believe me when I say that cleaning the garage is a Delight Blight for me!

Jeni likes order, structure and cleanliness. She also likes surprises. I have learned (not quickly) that unexpectedly sweeping the house for Jeni brings the Rapture Factor. I have learned that washing a load of towels, folding them and placing them neatly in the right drawers makes her very happy.

Since then, I have also learned the ways to bring enrichment to Jeni may change over the course of years. Today Jeni enjoys receiving cut flowers because our financial picture has changed. Today I can see the Rapture Factor when I give her cut flowers. I have learned to understand Jeni when she does not react the way I think she should. She has learned the same concept for me.

We can learn to accept individuals who are different from us. Learning this acceptance is a process and can reduce conflict in our stressed world.

We will now spend some time trying to learn the ways by which each of us find richness in life. It is yet one more way in which we have God-given differences.

IS PLEASURE A SIN?

Some Christians may ask "Is it wrong for us to have fulfillment, enjoyment, satisfaction and the Rapture Factor in this life?" Jesus said...

141

John 10:10: ...I am come that they might have life, and that they might have it more abundantly.

There is nothing more fulfilling in life than a close walk with Him. However, as people, since we do have flesh and blood, we have human needs. Our senses seek fulfillment. The world would tell us to please ourselves, but the Bible would tell us something different:

Romans 15:1-2: We then that are strong ought to bear the infirmities of the weak, and not to please ourselves. [2] Let every one of us please his neighbour for his good to edification.

The world would tell us we are number 1, but the New Testament tells us:

Mark 8:34: And when he (Jesus) had called the people unto him with his disciples also, he said unto them, Whosoever will come after me, let him deny himself, and take up his cross, and follow me.

The world would tell us to go to the head of the line, but the Word of God tells us:

Mark 9:35: And he sat down, and called the twelve, and saith unto them, If any man desire to be first, the same shall be last of all, and servant of all.

We find then, that God's way of looking at life is opposite from the world's standards. We do know each of us have certain things that give us greater fulfillment, satisfaction and gratification in life than others. Likewise, the Scripture tells us there are things which bring God fulfillment.

1 John 3:22: And whatsoever we ask, we receive of him, because we keep his commandments, and do those things that are pleasing in his sight.

Some things please God. Some do not. We are no different. Within each of us, buried in our personalities and in our innermost parts are unique needs waiting to be met.

Is it wrong to find enjoyment in viewing the Grand Canyon? Of course it is not. The Grand Canyon was created by Him for our pleasure. Is it wrong to find enjoyment in a wonderfully prepared meal? No, He gave us taste buds and the fruits of the Earth for our enjoyment and sustenance. Is it wrong to enjoy things that bring pleasure to our five senses of sight, hearing, smell, taste and touch? No, not unless they are expressly forbidden in the Scriptures.

God desires to be all things for us. He is able to meet all of our needs in a variety of ways.

PREFERENCES

One of my grandsons loves vegetables and fruit. He would choose a bag of carrots or a cluster of grapes before a candy bar. One of my grand-daughters loves anything that has a hint of chocolate, butter or sugar.

They find enjoyment or fulfillment in extremely different areas. Is one better than another? My dentist friend would tell me a definite "Yes"! But, these two grandchildren were raised by the same parents, yet each of these children has very different preferences even at the ages of six and eight.

When in a restaurant, our son Rick, looks at the menu to see what is available in two areas, chicken and fish. I immediately look for the beef section. Preferences that are different are neither wrong nor inappropriate.

A vacation to some people would mean traveling with friends. Others simply find ways of getting away by themselves.

143

Some love the mountains, while others love the beach. Some love the quiet, non-crowded areas, while others thrive in the populated places. We have many different preferences in life.

MISINTERPRETATIONS

As individuals, we can give and receive enrichment in our relationships with spouses or friends in a broad range of areas. We can also "miss the boat" entirely. For instance, a wife, with a strong melancholy personality, would be rather introverted, timid and shy. Because of these tendencies, the tenderness of holding hands with her husband may not be important to her.

However, her husband may derive great fulfillment from that contact. The lack of tenderness from her may cause him to believe he is unworthy of affection. It could affect his sense of self-worth, when, in fact, it is merely a difference of enrichment factors. What for him may be a Rapture Factor, for her may be a Delight Blight.

Jeni and I have very different enrichment areas. She is greatly pleased when I do things for her. Consequently, when I do a chore specifically for her, it clearly means that I love her.

Conversely, I receive no great pleasure when Jeni does chores for me. However, my enrichment lies in the tender areas of holding her hand or getting a hug. Those acts equate to an act of love for me.

STRETCHING EXERCISES

Sometimes to cope with the differences in our relationships with one another, we need to sacrifice our personal wishes and desires. While I get no personal enrichment or Rapture Factor by cleaning out our garage, I do it for Jeni. Likewise, she stretches herself to please me. Do you suppose it is those sacrifices which the Lord was referring to when he spoke of two people becoming one flesh?

144

I believe God would have us stretch ourselves to try and meet each other's needs when it is scripturally appropriate and applicable.

It is amazing to see how God stretches us in our relationships. Pairing us with spouses of opposite temperament, personality and enrichment factors keeps us from getting careless in our time together.

GETTING PRACTICE

As we seek to understand the differences among us, we learn to accept those who are different than us. Are our enrichment needs of any greater importance than anyone else's? The Bible teaches us our responsibility is to serve others and place them first. If that is the case, how should we best apply this concept of fulfillment and enrichment in our own lives and towards others?

When enrichment differences create conflicts, we have opportunities to resolve them. If the other person can understand our preferences and chooses to meet them, it is wonderful. But generally, we do not get the opportunity of voicing our preferences, much less having the privilege of having them met. Within our marriages and close friendships, we have those opportunities to communicate, but beyond that, it becomes less likely.

Thus, when we realize there are differences between us, we can learn to tolerate those who are different than us. We learn there are different preferences each individual has for things which enrich their lives. People have preferences, and that concept is certainly a God-given right. In many respects, it is not something learned. Those preferences are part of the gene package God placed within us, just like the carrot-loving grandson and the sugar-loving grand-daughter.

When we do not get our enrichment needs met by others, we can learn to grant them mercy. We realize they simply are different than we are. That can allow us to lower our expectations of others and thus reduce hurt feelings. There is a freedom that comes from this decision.

Have you ever wondered why some individuals seem to mimic a dynamite explosion when only a firecracker would have been sufficient? Sometimes there are hidden factors lurking under the surface providing additional fuel. The next chapter gives us some insight into some of those factors.

- 12 -

THE EMOTIONALLY CHALLENGED

THE CHALLENGED AMONG US

I had a situation arise several months ago when a man, whom I had known for many years, gave me a tongue lashing. It was very verbal, and it was very personal. However, I felt no defensiveness or hurt feelings. There was no anger. Was that because I have a handle on this issue of "coping with hurtful things"?

Not so, because I still need to work on this issue often. In this situation however, the "granting of mercy" to my verbal attacker happened automatically. I did not have to _try_ to grant mercy. Why?

The man, though middle-aged, has the mental capacity of an eight or ten year old. He was facing a difficult time in his life and I simply became a convenient outlet for his frustrations and confusion.

We seldom have a difficult time granting mercy towards those with mental challenges.

Recently, I was walking along a sidewalk to a restaurant. A lady was in front of me going through the doors. She acted as if she had the entire day to herself, and no one else had anyplace to go. She was so slow! Aggravating? No. The cane in her hand and her age automatically put her in the "let's grant her some mercy" category. We seldom have a difficult time "showing compassion" to those with physical and age related challenges.

149

If someone has a cane, a broken leg, a neck brace, or the physical appearance of having suffered a stroke, we are quick to give them the benefit of the doubt. We can also grant mercy and compassion quickly to those with a "wheelchair tag" hanging from their car mirror. We do not even need to think about granting mercy or showing compassion to those who outwardly have challenges.

However, what if someone has chronic back pain or their heart is operating at 50% capacity or they have another type of affliction that is not readily apparent? Granting mercy to those with maladies not so apparent comes with more difficulty, does it not?

EMOTIONAL CHALLENGES

The emotional handicaps of life are just as invisible at times as chronic back pain. When someone is abrasive to us, are we quick to wonder if they have some hurtful emotional issue in their life they are dealing with? Generally, we are not. Rather, we might be quick to take things personally and become defensive and lash out at the person.

We will now try to identify those emotional things that make us different from each other. Remember, differences can either be avenues to conflict or opportunities for reaching out to others.

Let us explore how to cope with those who handle their emotions differently than we do. Who has the authority to say what is normal and what is not, when the issue of emotions come up?

WHAT DOES THE BIBLE SAY?

The Bible tells us clearly we are made in the likeness of God, helping us to understand we are like Him in every way, including the emotional sense. Those emotions we feel, both positive and negative, He experiences as well. We do not need to search the Bible too deeply to find instances of God's joy and love, as well as His anger, hurt, jealousy and disappointment.

Ezekiel 36:5: Therefore thus saith the Lord God; Surely in the fire of my jealousy have I spoken against the residue of the heathen...

Mark 3:5: And when he (Jesus) had looked round about on them with anger, being grieved for the hardness of their hearts...

At what point do our emotions leave the normal realm and enter the inappropriate realm? The Bible gives us some clear indications:

Ephesians 4:26: Be ye angry, and sin not: let not the sun go down upon your wrath.

Ephesians 4:31: Let all bitterness, and wrath, and anger, and clamor, and evil speaking, be put away from you, with all malice.

Titus 3:3: For we ourselves also were sometimes foolish, disobedient, deceived, serving divers lusts and pleasures, living in malice and envy, hateful, and hating one another.

Psalms 97:10: Ye that love the Lord, hate evil...

Proverbs 14:30: A sound heart is the life of the flesh: but envy the rottenness of the bones.

Based upon the Bible, there are appropriate times for anger and jealousy, but certainly not appropriate times for lust. Are there appropriate times for hatred? The Bible assures us there most certainly are. God had jealousy when His children served other gods. Jesus felt anger while mankind was defiling the

151

temple. A hatred for sin and satan is an appropriate attitude for a Christian Believer. The Bible identifies the difference between sin and the expression of healthy emotions.

This chapter on the *emotionally challenged* among us deals with those who have not learned the difference between appropriate and inappropriate ways of handling emotions. It also deals with those who were taught a warped emotional response in how to deal with emotions.

DO UNTO OTHERS...

Can we say we have full control over our emotions? Can we say we handle all things appropriately? If we feel defensive and have hurt feelings when someone hurts us, we probably do have some unresolved issues.

Do we want others to grant us mercy or give us the benefit of the doubt when we fail to have an appropriate emotional response? If so, then we have the responsibility of giving them the same mercy when they fail us.

In Chapter 9, we discussed the many types of backgrounds and experiences which create issues in our lives. We learned those past experiences sometimes cause us to react negatively towards other people due to stress, fears and the realities of life.

When we handle those experiences in negative ways, are we emotionally challenged? Possibly so. If we find ourselves imperfect, what should our reaction be to those who react wrongfully to us? The Word tells us:

Luke 6:31: ...as ye would that men should do to you, do ye also to them likewise.

ENABLING

A term commonly used in the areas of social work, mental health, and emotional health is "enabling." Enabling is the concept of encouraging others to continue their inappropriate behavior.

For instance, it is used to describe how some people through their actions, inactions or words can inadvertently encourage an alcoholic or drug addict to continue their damaging and self-destructive behavior.

Enabling occurs in situations when we have an inappropriate response to someone's sins, such as:

- It's OK. This was my fault, not yours.
- You acted appropriately.
- Everyone would have handled this just as you did.
- You are justified in how you feel.

None of these responses will encourage change. We can be most helpful by reacting with appropriate emotional reactions. We are unable to minister to hurting people if we are frustrated, angry or bitter towards them. Granting them mercy gets our own emotions out of the way and gives us an opportunity for ministering with love to their needs. I appreciate the verse:

1 Peter 4:8: And above all things have fervent charity among yourselves: for charity shall cover the multitude of sins.

When I speak of granting mercy or compassion to someone who is behaving badly, I am not talking about enabling them. There is a fine line. Thinking through the following questions should help determine an appropriate attitude and motive:

- Is it my responsibility to correct or fix this person?
- Do I know all there is to know about this person's background and experiences of life?
- Have I dealt appropriately with the issues in my life which have contributed to this conflict?

- What is the worst and best thing that could happen if I do not challenge this person's behavior?
- What is the best and worst thing which could happen if I do challenge this person's behavior?

THE RIGHT PROCESS

When we are hurt by someone else's quick words or actions, we first need to ask ourselves some tough questions:

- Am I quick to justify my hurt?
- Do I want to retaliate?
- Am I quick to pity myself?
- Am I searching for revenge?

If we find our answers to any of those questions are "yes," then we need to challenge our own thinking patterns. It would be good to channel our thinking down these lines:

- This person may have had some serious hurt in their life.
- Possibly this person has been through some traumatic experiences I do not know about.
- Something else must be wrong to have caused this person to act or react so inappropriately.

It is not too difficult to believe the people around us have hidden hurts, such as; unresolved grief, unrealized expectations, a disrupted relationship, a child in the hospital, or an illness we do not know about. Each of us has a difficult time living and dealing with tough issues in our life. When we can assume others are going through tough times as well, it is easier to grant them mercy, compassion and grace.

Sometimes we witness an unusual reaction to a situation from someone. What could possibly have caused them to react in such a bizarre manner? They seem normal in every other respect. Could there be some issue impacting this? The next chapter explores how fears may cause us to react to some things in odd ways.

- 13 -

FEARS

BEAR FEARS

In 1996, Jeni, our son Rick and I spent some time in the Teton mountain range of Wyoming. The three of us did the usual short and not so tough hikes, but Rick and I decided to do an off-trail hike to a glacier. As we left the parking lot at the trailhead we saw a warning sign about bears. That brought an immediate fear to me, but it quickly went away as I thought about the minimal likelihood of running across a bear in the wild.

Having left the trail, Rick was about fifty feet ahead of me as we were cutting across a wooded ridge on the way up to the glacier. All of a sudden, he stopped! When I caught up with him he pointed downhill to a grizzly bear with two cubs about 100 feet away!

Immediately, I felt fear and a surge of adrenaline! Not just because I was seeing a wild grizzly, but because she was only 100 feet away with two cubs! I had read many accounts of grizzly attacks and knew the chances of escaping or surviving an attack was minimal. A close encounter with a grizzly bear and her cubs made survival inconceivable.

The fear was intense for me, (Rick however, was enjoying the encounter.) I knew enough about bear behavior to know you do not, under any circumstance, maintain eye contact with a grizzly in the wild. However, because the fear was so intense, it was impossible to look away. I was captivated by the sight. The standoff lasted for about 20 seconds until she bit one of the cubs and chased him into the brush. Then, they all disappeared. Everything seemed deathly quiet in those next few seconds!

I just knew without a doubt the bear was circling and it would only be a matter of seconds until she came barreling out of the brush at us. But, thanks to an awesome God who protects us in spite of ourselves, we saw her disappearing over a ridge 100 yards away. The fear started to slowly dissipate, and in spite of Rick's wishes to follow her, we headed for the car.

CHIHUAHUA FEARS

People are surprised when they see me, at 6 foot and 190 pounds, back up when confronted by a small Chihuahua dog. In fact, I recently needed to pick something up at a place of business outside of town. On the way there, I was annoyed with myself for not having asked the shop owner if he had a dog. So, when I got there and saw a doghouse with no dog around, I was apprehensive (actually scared) about getting out of the car. If I would have seen a chained dog, I would have felt better. But an empty doghouse usually indicates a dog is around somewhere. Not being able to see a dog made me feel that one was lurking in the shadows just waiting for my tender leg to exit my car.

My hands did their usual sweaty palm trick...

Fear is relative and has its different levels. I was afraid to appear "chicken" in front of the shop owner. However, even more of a profound fear was that I did not want a dog attached to my leg. So I did the chicken thing.

I called the shop owner with my cell phone from my car in his driveway. So, from 50 feet away I asked him if he had a dog. He did not, so I went into his shop, relieved. He thought this was all a bit funny (actually really funny). But, when I told him I had been bitten by a German Shepherd named Rip when I

158

was ten, he apologized for laughing at me. Immediately, he became sympathetic because he now understood my fear.

CONSEQUENCES OF FEAR

My experience with the grizzly along with the memories and the fears associated with her, could keep me away from Yellowstone, Glacier National Park, and the Canadian Rockies. My desire to experience life in its richness can outweigh those fears, and I may be able to go to those places and experience His creation again.

I find it utterly amazing how we allow fears to dictate our lives. Isn't it astounding how fears can rob us of joy, happiness and the abundant life?

SLEEPING BEARS

How many fears do we have hibernating within us? When winter gives way to spring, we know bears come out of hibernation. Similarly, when hurtful situations occur to us, our fears emerge. The fears within us rise, and our defense mechanisms claw their way to the surface.

We become angry and defensive. Our lives are centered on our fear. The fear becomes the object on which our eyes and emotions are glued. Nothing else seems to matter. We simply cannot separate ourselves from our fear. Just as I was powerless to look away from the grizzly, it is virtually impossible to get our focus off our fears.

FEAR FOCUS

Since you are now aware of my childhood dog-biting incident, I believe you will understand if you see me back up from a small tail-wagging Chihuahua dog. You will understand why I show fear.

Just recently as I was getting out of my car in a parking lot, a dog on a leash being walked by an elderly lady barked. I physically jumped! She looked at me and smiled a gracious smile. I knew what she was thinking, "How can such a big man be afraid of a little Schnauzer?" I felt compelled to tell her about my experience with "Rip." After listening, she smiled and I knew she understood my fear.

How many strange behaviors or actions do we not understand about others? Is it possible they may be responding to fears they feel from their own experiences with "dogs, bears or whatever"? By presuming so, we can grant mercy much more quickly to others who hurt us or are treating us in an unusual way. We can assume and believe they may have underlying, hidden reasons for their different behavior.

The bear and dog issues bring emotions from deep within me that are typical of reactionary fear. They are easily defined and can be easily understood by others when explained. However, there are other fears within us that are not so easily defined and certainly not easily explained to others. They are, nevertheless, just as intense. Can we give others the benefit of the doubt when they react in seemingly inappropriate ways to small things?

Two of the most dominant fears most of us have are; a fear of failing (not being good enough) and a fear of being rejected. If we have a fear of failing or not measuring up, we will have different responses to life situations than someone who does not have that fear of failure. If we have a fear of someone rejecting us, we again will have different responses to life situations than someone who lacks that fear. Those two fears bring defensive mechanisms and reactions which may easily hurt others.

IS EVERYONE AFFLICTED BY FEAR?

As you recall my personal story in Chapter 1, you will not be surprised to know I tend to struggle with a fear of being rejected. Having lived with rejection during those first 17 years of my life has had its impact.

Jeni lives with a fear of failure. Her personality, background experiences, and gifts take her down the path of wanting to do things "just right."

Being human, we are each unique and prone to certain fears. When we are able to identify our fears, we will be able to predict how we will react to certain future situations. This can give us some control over our ability to act and react appropriately to hurtful situations.

SETTING BOUNDARIES

It is important to learn how to set up boundaries. I will not hike on trails where there is a sign indicating the presence of a bear. I stay away from places which have dogs, unless I know the owner of the dog is present. Boundaries are helpful in dealing with our fears. However, fears can be so dominant they can dictate and control our lives.

Sometimes the fear of dirt and bacteria is so strong, people can be obsessed with cleanliness and can allow this obsession to dominate their lives.

Some people have a fear of becoming obese. Their resultant eating habits can destroy their health and sometimes their lives.

In our mission to minimize our hurts by feeling compassion for others, we can be helped by looking at some imaginary people in hypothetical situations where fear is the controlling factor.

BOB AND SUE

Bob and Sue have been married for fifteen years. Their three children mean the world to them. Sue was raised in a family where she never quite lived up to her mother's expectations. The never-ending failure she felt growing up created a fear of failure in Sue's life.

Bob and Sue have a twelve year old daughter named Tiffany. Because of Sue's fear of failing, she keeps a tight hold on Tiffany's life. Sue never allows Tiffany to participate in extracurricular activities. Sue has many reasons and excuses as to why Tiffany can not participate.

But, underlying it all, Sue's thoughts were, "What if Tiffany fails? Won't that make me look like a failure?" Sue's husband, Bob, is very frustrated as he sees Sue's fears starting to alienate Tiffany. The fear of failing for Sue not only stifles her life, but that of her daughter. Fears restrict us, as well as those around us.

BRAD AND CINDY

Brad and Cindy have been married for eight years. Their eight years together have been rather stormy. Brad's father deserted his family when Brad was ten years old. Brad never quite got over feeling responsible for his dad leaving and felt very rejected throughout his teen years. He reasoned in his young mind, "It is only natural for a dad and his son to do things together. There must be some things about me Dad did not like. I must have done something wrong for him to leave me."

Those feelings of rejection clouded Brad's future relationships like a San Francisco fog. Cindy has complained that Brad never was able to talk about what he was feeling. He was always so busy with "things" they could not talk about "themselves." Their emotional intimacy could not get off the ground.

Brad's continued fear of rejection stopped him short of developing any kind of deep relationship. The thought, "If I get close, this person will reject me," was always in the back of his mind. In fact, Brad would do things to sabotage close relationships. Brad reasoned, "If I step back from them first, they will not have the chance to walk away from me." The fear of rejection for Brad not only stifles his life, but that of his wife.

Fear restricts and interferes with our relationships to those around us.

PUTTING IT TOGETHER

Bob and Sue - When Bob was able to understand Sue's childhood, he began to understand her controlling and manipulative nature. He could understand her fear of failing. He became more perceptive of her fears and began to not take things as personally. When Bob was able to get his own emotions out of the way, he could reach out to Sue and give her reassurances of his unconditional love. That unconditional love paved the way for trust and healing of her hurtful past.

Brad and Cindy - It took Cindy some time to understand what Brad had gone through as a child. Since he was reluctant to talk about what he was feeling, she drew wrong conclusions. Originally, she had felt there must be something wrong with her since Brad would not get "close." However, when Cindy began to realize she was not the reason for Brad's withdrawal or his lack of emotional intimacy, their relationship grew.

When she could understand his issues of early rejection, she could have compassion and pity on him and could assure him of her unconditional love. Who among us does not respond to unconditional love? Over time, when Brad saw Cindy was committed to him, he responded with more emotional intimacy. When Cindy got her own emotions out of the way, she could reach out to Brad and give him the reassurances he needed. She could not do that until she realized she was not the problem and started feeling compassion for Brad.

When we can show compassion, mercy and unconditional love to those bound in fear, positive results are usually just around the corner.

Fears get in the way of the abundant life Jesus promised the born-again Believer. An appropriate Bible verse that summarizes this particular chapter is:

1 John 4:18: There is no fear in love; but perfect love casteth out fear...

In the next chapter, we will consider an issue which, at first glance, may seem unusual. The issue is a concept centering on the definitions of "love" versus "like". As we study this area, we simply find another area of life in which each of us is uniquely different.

LOVE vs. LIKE

When I was in the fourth grade, a girl in my class captured my attention. I do not know why or how it started. Possibly it was a Valentine's card, a smile - who knows? That was over four decades ago! In any case, since I "liked" her, I thought "love" must just be up the scale a bit, or so it seemed to my fourth grade emotional mind. Therefore I was operating on the premise that if I "like" someone, and things are going well, "love" is just around the corner. Or is it?

We seem to start out in life believing "*like*" and "*love*" are on the same barometer, scale or thermometer. We tend to think we will start with a "like" emotion and move towards a "love" emotion. However, there is another point of view to consider.

Consider "like" and "love" as two very separate issues but having indirect ties. Think of them as being on two different scales. Comparing the two would be like comparing apples and oranges. Having one does not guarantee the presence of the other. We may experience both at the same time for the same person, but that is not necessarily the case.

SATAN'S ADVANTAGE

Satan is very much aware of our tendency to put love and like on the same scale. He uses the single scale concept to his advantage.

Since we are Biblically commanded to "love" everyone, we may feel judged by God if we do not "like" everyone. Thus, according to satan's theology, he makes us think we can not love others if we do not first like them. Can you see how satan might use this to his advantage? He is the great accuser.

There are probably things about me that are difficult for some people to like. My personality perhaps? The manner in which I get irritable when I do plumbing? My indecisiveness? There are times I am not a very likable person. A toothache, headache, carving a turkey or a plumbing job can make me grouchy and irritable. Those are not "likable" traits.

I have mentioned earlier that Jeni and I are extreme opposites in the areas of personality, spiritual gifts, enrichment and background. In our 35 years of marriage, we have always loved each other very much. There have been times, because of our differences, when we have not liked each other as much. Satan could *try* to accuse us of not loving each other, but he has not been able to use that wedge with us. "Love" has never been an issue between us. However, the concept of "like" is an entirely different matter and is important to consider.

Our goal in this chapter is to reduce the power of satan when he condemns us or accuses us of not loving each other. We will seek to learn this by understanding the difference between "*like*" and "*love*".

AN ODD TITLE

A title such as ***Love versus Like*** must stir up some type of curiosity. As Christian Believers we certainly have an understanding of the concept of the term "love." Over the years, most of us have realized the differences between statements such as, "I love hot dogs" and, "I love my wife." If we do not see much of a difference between the two, then marital counseling may be in order.

In any case, a study of the definition of the words related to "love" in the Greek language has been able to help us understand the different "types" of love. The word "love" in the King James

Version of the Bible actually represents several types of love. There are instances of sacrificial love, affectionate love, friend love and some variations thereof.

The Bible is specific in many places in commanding us to "love":

Matthew 22:37: Jesus said unto him, Thou shalt love the Lord thy God with all thy heart, and with all thy soul, and with all thy mind.

Matthew 22:39: Thou shalt love thy neighbor as thyself.

Ephesians 5:25: Husbands, love your wives, even as Christ also loved the church, and gave himself for it.

John 15:12: This is my commandment, That ye love one another, as I have loved you.

WHAT ARE WE FEELING?

It is important to note that the Scripture does not give us options of loving one another and of loving God. Without any doubt, we are commanded to love. Since we are all aware of the scriptural commandments of "loving," how do we deal with feelings other than love for someone else? What is the emotion we are feeling when we have a negative reaction toward someone? What is the emotion we feel when someone has made us defensive or has hurt our feelings? Is it hate? Is it bitterness? Is it resentment? Are these words associated with love? At what point do we stop loving someone in a Scriptural way?

These are excellent questions to consider as we deal with the concept of granting mercy to those who are quite different than us.

Satan is always looking for ways in which
he may accuse the Believer.

Revelation 12:10: And I heard a loud voice saying in heaven, Now is come salvation, and strength, and the kingdom of our God, and the power of his Christ: for the accuser of our brethren is cast down, which accused them before our God day and night.

Can you imagine satan's accusations against someone who is struggling in their ability to like someone else?

"You call yourself a Believer and you do not _like_ Linda? The Bible commands you to _love_ everyone. How can you call yourself a born-again Christian if you do not _like_ her?"

Satan has convinced some of us that liking someone is synonymous with loving someone. Let us consider another way of looking at this subject.

Most of us would agree the opposite of love is hate. The original Greek in the New Testament identifies hate with words such as; detest, enmity and persecution. The dictionary defines hate with words such as disgust, loathing, hostility, abhorrence, repugnant and aversion.

What is the opposite of the term "like"? Could we agree the opposite is "dislike"? The Bible does not use the word "like" in the terms with which we are speaking. Rather it uses words such as: delight, pleasure and enjoy.

There are Bible verses to indicate that God has preferences for some things over others:

Hebrews 10:38: Now the just shall live by faith: but if any man draw back, my soul shall have no _pleasure_ in him.

The original Greek for "pleasure" in this verse describes it as being pleasing; being affectionate towards; and finding delight in. There are things God finds pleasure in, as well as things He finds no pleasure in.

Jeremiah 9:24: But let him that glorieth glory in this, that he understandeth and knoweth me, that I am the Lord which exercise lovingkindness, judgment, and righteousness, in the earth: for in these things I *delight*, saith the Lord.

The original Hebrew for "delight" in this verse describes it as: being pleasing, finding pleasure in and finding favor. The verse is an example of something God does like. In the Jeremiah verse as well as the Hebrews verse, the word "love" is not used. We thus can draw the conclusion there is a difference between love and like.

The term "like" is synonymous with words like appreciation, enjoyment, satisfaction and pleasing.

We like being with people who are similar to us. We enjoy being with people who make us feel comfortable and are not demanding. We find pleasure in being with people who enjoy being with us. We appreciate being with people who have the same hobbies as we do. We delight in being with people who have the same convictions as we do. These are all basic "like" statements. What is the opposite of the term "like"?

The opposite would be "dislike." The scale for "love" ranges from love to hate. The scale for "like" runs from like to dislike. Love and like are on two separate scales. Satan would have us believe they are on the same scale. The Bible *does* command us to "love" one another. The Bible *does not* command us to "like" one another. The Bible gives us freedom to enjoy and appreciate things and people on different levels just as God does.

EXTREMES

Of course, anything can be taken out of context and taken to an extreme. The Bible does give us the right to prefer certain things above other things. The Bible gives us the privilege to enjoy and appreciate certain people over others. However, the Bible commands us to not show partiality among people. Partiality would be the inappropriate concept of giving undue advantage to one person over another. James, Chapter 2, deals with this issue in a very direct way. It deals with how we treat people, things we do for them, and specifically where we would have them sit at a banquet.

We need to understand it is permissible to have varying degrees of "like" that are not related to the concept of "love." These differences can be shown by the following thoughts:

- I really like being around Joe. His personality and mine seem to connect.
- I do not like being with Jim. Our personalities tend to clash. It is difficult for me to be around him.
- I like the way I feel when I am with Linda. She has such a positive attitude.
- I like being with Rita. She has a unique way of taking a real life situation and bringing a spiritual truth from it.
- I really love Brad, but he is not an easy person to like right now.
- My wife and I are best friends. Not only do I love her, I also really like her.

There are some people who simply irritate or frustrate us more than other people. They can hurt us and make us defensive.

172

God is not commanding us to like the ways in which these people hurt us, nor is He commanding us to "like" being around them.

In Chapter 3 we talked about the "realities of life." Reality means there are those who can get under our skin more quickly than others. Reality means there are personality types which can be abrasive to us. We are not required to be best friends with them. However, God does command us to love them.

The purpose of this chapter has been to rob satan of some of his accusatory and condemning power by replacing it with truth. When he accuses us of not loving someone, we need to determine what the true issue is. Is the issue really "love," or is it a "like" issue? We need to remind ourselves "love" is commanded and "like" is a preference. The concept allows us to grant mercy to others when we are hurt by them.

God is not asking us to have everyone as a best friend. In fact, we will not enjoy going out to dinner with everyone. We will always have our preferences.

- 15 -

WHAT NOW?

There is an old saying, "Where there is breath, there is life." We could add to that and say, "Where there is life, there is hurt." Unless we live as a hermit, the reality of life is quite simple - we *will* be hurt by others. Perfect strangers *will* show us disrespect and dishonor. Co-workers *will* play the politics game, and we *will* find our fingers stepped on by others scrambling up the ladder of success. The number of hurts in our lives will be in direct proportion to the number of days we have yet to live and the number of people we brush shoulders with. How could it be otherwise?

Relationships with others will bring fulfillment, enrichment, joy, happiness and contentment. Relationships with others will also bring hurt. If we gamble nothing in a relationship, we gain nothing in return.

Learning coping skills in living can minimize the hurts of life. Learning about our uniquely created differences can increase our understanding of one another. Utilizing that understanding can promote compassion for others. This compassion can allow us to give others the benefit of the doubt. By giving others the benefit of the doubt, we can grant them mercy and forgiveness. What are the results of dealing with hurt in a healthy way? We have peace of mind.

None of this is possible without the healing power of the Holy Spirit. It is an impossible task without the Word, prayer and His marvelous grace and strength. When we use God's resources, we can each experience the abundant life God has promised to His children.

- 16 -

WORKBOOK

Progress brings hope. Hope brings progress. Fortunately for those of us trying to deal with hurt, growth can be measured. One method of monitoring improvement is to quantify how you are doing compared to a set of standards.

Following are seven general categories of issues we have dealt with in the preceding chapters. As you take the same tests periodically, you will be able to see growth as your attitudes change. At the end of the seven tests are sections where you may record your results by date for future and ongoing comparison.

The seven categories are:

- Self Worth
- My Perception of God
- Guilt and Blame
- My Character
- My Relationships
- Forgiveness
- Fears

Each of the tests has 10 statements. Consider each one and how it may pertain to your life. Place the appropriate number in the blanks preceding the statement. The total will give you an idea of how you are dealing with that particular issue.

Self-Worth

1 = always
2 = often
3 = half the time
4 = seldom
5 = never

_____ I have a poor sense of self-worth.

_____ I do not like who I am.

_____ I hate myself.

_____ There are things about myself for which I feel shame.

_____ It is difficult for me to accept a compliment.

_____ I feel if people really knew me, they would not like me.

_____ I pity myself.

_____ I want pity from others.

_____ I feel I have nothing to offer others.

_____ I wonder what others think about me.

_____ *TOTAL*

Self-Worth - _Scoring Key_

0 to 20 – Your life is dominated by your negative perception of who and what you are. Many of your decisions and reactions in life are clouded by these images of who and what you are.

21 to 30 – There are still issues and factors in your life which affect your ability to live the abundant life. While life is manageable, greater joy and happiness will be the result of your efforts.

31 to 40 – While there is room for improvement, your self-worth is relatively healthy. You will have issues which arise; however, over time you can deal with them.

41 to 50 – You have an above average sense of who and what you are.

My Perception of God

1 = always
2 = often
3 = half the time
4 = seldom
5 = never

_____ I doubt God loves me unconditionally.

_____ I doubt God likes me.

_____ I doubt my salvation.

_____ God seems like a harsh taskmaster.

_____ God is not merciful, kind and loving.

_____ God shows partiality and favoritism among people.

_____ God demands perfection from me.

_____ God does not hear me when I pray.

_____ God is displeased with me.

_____ I fear eternal judgment.

_____ *TOTAL*

My Perception of God - *Scoring Key*

0 to 20 – Your perception of God is not Biblically accurate. Your vision of Him is negative rather than positive and affects your relationship with Him as well as with others.

21 to 30 – There are still issues and factors in your life which affect your ability to view God in a healthy way. While life is manageable, greater joy and happiness will be the result of your efforts to know Him in a more personal way.

31 to 40 – While there is room for improvement, your overall perception of God is healthy. You will have issues which arise; however, with time you will be able to deal with them.

41 to 50 – You have an above average sense of who and what God is to you. Your relationship with Him is personal and close.

_____

Guilt and Blame

1 = always
2 = often
3 = half the time
4 = seldom
5 = never

_____ I feel guilt even though I am repentant.

_____ I blame God when bad things happen.

_____ I blame people when bad things happen.

_____ I blame myself when bad things happen.

_____ God should use Old Testament judgment with sinners.

_____ I get defensive when someone challenges me.

_____ I justify my mistakes.

_____ People deserve to be punished when they fail.

_____ God is waiting for me to do something wrong.

_____ God is quick to condemn and slow to show mercy.

_____ _TOTAL_

Guilt and Blame - *Scoring Key*

0 to 20 – Your life is dominated by guilt. To reduce the heavy load of guilt you are carrying, you tend to blame others. It damages your relationship with others because they sense your judgment.

21 to 30 – There are still issues and factors in your life which affect your ability to live beyond guilt and blame. While life is manageable, greater joy and happiness will be the result of your efforts to reduce guilt and blame in yourself and with others.

31 to 40 – While guilt is something you carry occasionally, you are able to deal with it over the course of time.

41 to 50 – You have an above average sense of who and what the Holy Spirit is and what He means to you.

My Character

1 = always
2 = often
3 = half the time
4 = seldom
5 = never

_____ I am a controlling person.

_____ I manipulate people to get my way.

_____ I manipulate circumstances to get my way.

_____ I am always right.

_____ I have to do things myself to make sure they are done
correctly.

_____ I have no patience for those who make mistakes.

_____ I am a selfish person.

_____ I am a jealous person.

_____ I am an envious person.

_____ I cannot understand people who do not help
themselves.

_____ *TOTAL*

My Character - *Scoring Key*

0 to 20 – Overall, your life has many areas of hurt. However, as you begin to understand and learn to deal with the differences among us as people, you will see positive results and improvement in your score on this test.

21 to 30 – There are still issues and factors in your life which mold and shape your character in negative ways. While life is manageable, greater joy and happiness will be the result of your efforts to look beyond yourself and towards the needs of others.

31 to 40 – While there is room for improvement, your character is relatively normal. You will have issues which arise; however, with time you will be able to deal with them.

41 to 50 – You have an above average ability to deal with negative factors in your life. You appear to have a close relationship with God and know His grace.

My Relationships

1 = always
2 = often
3 = half the time
4 = seldom
5 = never

_____ I never have close friends.

_____ I do not want close friends.

_____ People hurt me when they get close.

_____ I cannot trust people.

_____ People think I am a cold person.

_____ People think I am distant.

_____ I am no one's best friend.

_____ My good relationships with others eventually turn
    sour.

_____ I fear being rejected by people.

_____ I stop relationships early so the other person does not
    have a chance to reject me later.

_____ *TOTAL*

My Relationships - _Scoring Key_

0 to 20 – Your life is dominated by a fear of being rejected by others. That fear keeps you from having close relationships and causes you to be sad and possibly depressed.

21 to 30 – There are still issues and factors in your life which affect your ability to have healthy relationships with others. While life is manageable, greater joy and happiness will be the result of your efforts to allow others into your life.

31 to 40 – While there is room for improvement, your relationships with others are relatively normal. You will have issues which arise; however, with time you can deal with them.

41 to 50 – You have an above average ability to develop and maintain meaningful relationships.

Forgiveness

1 = always
2 = often
3 = half the time
4 = seldom
5 = never

_____ It is difficult for me to forgive those who hurt me.

_____ I carry grudges for lengthy periods of time.

_____ I want God to punish those who hurt me.

_____ I want to punish those who hurt me.

_____ People must say "I am sorry" before I can forgive
them.

_____ People who fail are unworthy of my love.

_____ People who sin are unworthy of God's love.

_____ I have difficulty forgiving myself when I fail.

_____ When I fail at the same thing multiple times, I am
unworthy of forgiveness even though I am repentant.

_____ I am harsh with those who sin.

_____ *TOTAL*

Forgiveness - _Scoring Key_

0 to 20 – Your life is dominated by your own failure, as well as the failure of others. You are quick to identify negative issues in yourself as well as others. You lack in the ability to forgive and grant mercy.

21 to 30 – There are still issues and factors in your life which affect your ability to forgive yourself and others. While life is manageable, greater joy and happiness will be the result of your efforts to grant mercy.

31 to 40 – While there is room for improvement, your understanding of forgiveness is normal. You will have issues which arise; however, with time you will be able to deal with them.

41 to 50 – You have an above average sense of mercy, grace and forgiveness.

Fears

1 = always
2 = often
3 = half the time
4 = seldom
5 = never

_____ I fear getting close to other people.

_____ I fear giving love because it may not be returned.

_____ I try really hard to get people to like me.

_____ I will go out of my way to have people accept me.

_____ I fear trying new things.

_____ I fear failure.

_____ I am a perfectionist.

_____ I fear other people's failures can make me look bad if
those people are my responsibility.

_____ I fear God will punish me for wrongdoing.

_____ I fear those I love will be taken away.

_____ *TOTAL*

190

Fears - *Scoring Key*

0 to 20 – Your life is dominated by multiple fears. Those fears have dramatically reduced your ability to experience the abundant life. Some of the fears possibly have become an obsession.

21 to 30 – There are still issues and factors in your life which affect your ability to live beyond fear. While life is manageable, greater joy and happiness will be the result of your efforts to confront your fears.

31 to 40 – While there is room for improvement, you have a relatively healthy control of the fears in your life. You will have issues which arise; however, with time you can deal with them.

41 to 50 – You have an above average control over the fears in your life. You understand God's power and control over His creation.

Enter the totals for each Test category in the appropriate blanks below. Take the tests in the seven categories periodically to determine your progress. There are five additional scoring sections for you to record future answers.

Date _____

Self-Worth   _____
My Perception of God   _____
Guilt and Blame   _____
My Character   _____
My Relationships   _____
Forgiveness   _____
Fears   _____

            TOTAL   _____

_____

Date _____

Self-Worth   _____
My Perception of God   _____
Guilt and Blame   _____
My Character   _____
My Relationships   _____
Forgiveness   _____
Fears   _____

TOTAL   _____

Date _____

Self-Worth   _____
My Perception of God   _____
Guilt and Blame   _____
My Character   _____
My Relationships   _____
Forgiveness   _____
Fears   _____

TOTAL   _____

Date _____

Self-Worth   _____
My Perception of God   _____
Guilt and Blame   _____
My Character   _____
My Relationships   _____
Forgiveness   _____
Fears   _____

TOTAL   _____

Date _____

Self-Worth   _____
My Perception of God   _____
Guilt and Blame   _____
My Character   _____
My Relationships   _____
Forgiveness   _____
Fears   _____

        TOTAL   _____

Date _____

Self-Worth   _____
My Perception of God   _____
Guilt and Blame   _____
My Character   _____
My Relationships   _____
Forgiveness   _____
Fears   _____

        TOTAL   _____